CW00484908

BTEC Tech Award

There's a lot to cover in the BTEC Tech Award in Sport, but don't worry
— help is at hand from the revision experts!

This brilliant CGP Revision Guide is full of clear and concise explanations for every
component of the course. There are also plenty of top tips and advice for the exam
and assignments, all in CGP's classic style. It's a winner!

Unlock your Online Edition

Just scan the QR code below or go to **cgpbooks.co.uk/extras** and enter this code!

3448 2244 2392 3095

By the way, this code only works for one person. If somebody else has
used this book before you, they might have already claimed the code.

Revision Guide

Contents

Published by CGP

Editors: Helen Clements, Liam Dyer, Sharon Keeley-Holden, Alison Palin, James Summersgill, Adam Worster

Reviewers: Chris Cope, Jenny Dobbyn and Joanna Hicks

With thanks to Glenn Rogers and Camilla Sheridan for the proofreading.

With thanks to Alice Dent for the copyright research.

Learning Outcomes wording on page 2 reproduced with permission of Pearson Education Ltd.

Physical Activity data on pages 8-9 © Crown copyright 2019. Licensed under the Open Government Licence v3.0.
http://nationalarchives.gov.uk/doc/open-government-licence/version/3/

The scale on page 52 is the Borg RPE scale® (© Gunnar Borg, 1970, 1998, 2017). Scale printed with permission.
The scale and full instruction can be obtained through BorgPerception www.borgperception.se

Normative data table for grip dynamometer test on page 72 was published in 'Physical Education and the Study of Sport' 4th ed, 2002, Davis ed, p.123, 1 table ('Normative data table for grip strength test' for 16 to 19 year olds), Copyright Elsevier (2023).

ISBN: 978 1 83774 061 1
Printed by Elanders Ltd, Newcastle upon Tyne.
Graphics from Corel® and Getty PA

Text, design, layout and original illustrations © Coordination Group Publications Ltd (CGP) 2023
All rights reserved.

Based on the classic CGP style created by Richard Parsons.

Photocopying more than one section of this book is not permitted, even if you have a CLA licence.
Extra copies are available from CGP with next day delivery • 0800 1712 712 • www.cgpbooks.co.uk

Course Overview

You don't need to be in the dark about <u>BTEC Sport</u> — this page will shine a light on everything you will face.

The Course is Split into Three Components

Component 1: Preparing Participants to Take Part in Sport and Physical Activity

Component 1 is divided into <u>three parts</u> (A, B, C):

- A: Explore types and provision of sport and physical activity for different types of participant.
- B: Examine equipment and technology required for participants to use when taking part in sport and physical activity.
- C: Be able to prepare participants to take part in sport and physical activity.

> These parts are also called 'learning outcomes'.

Your <u>teacher</u> will give you an <u>assignment</u> to complete <u>under supervision in class</u>. It will have <u>three tasks</u>:

Task	Part	Time	Marks
1	A	2 hours	24
2	B	1 hour	12
3	C	2 hours	24

> Component 1 is worth 30% of your total grade.

Component 2: Taking Part and Improving Other Participants' Sporting Performance

Component 2 is divided into three parts (A, B, C):

- A: Understand how different components of fitness are used in different physical activities.
- B: Be able to participate in sport and understand the roles and responsibilities of officials.
- C: Demonstrate ways to improve participants' sporting techniques.

> Component 2 is worth 30% of your total grade.

Your teacher will give you an assignment to complete <u>under supervision in class</u>. It will have four tasks:

Task	Part	Time	Marks
1	A	1 hour	12
2	B	1 hour	12
3	B	1 hour	12
4	C	1 hour	24

> In task 4, you'll need to produce video evidence of skills, including specific guidance and teaching points.

Component 3: Developing Fitness to Improve Other Participants' Performance in Sport and Physical Activity

> Component 3 is worth 40% of your total grade.

Component 3 is divided into four parts (A, B, C, D):

- A: Explore the importance of fitness for sports performance.
- B: Investigate fitness testing to determine fitness levels.
- C: Investigate different fitness training methods.
- D: Investigate fitness programming to improve fitness and sports performance.

For this component, you'll sit an exam worth 60 marks. It lasts 1 hour and 30 minutes.

> See pages 91-92 for more on the exam.

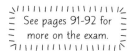

Types of Sport

First, you need to know the <u>definition</u> of a <u>sport</u> and the <u>different types</u> of sport that exist.

Sport is Physical Activity with Rules

1) A <u>sport</u> is a <u>competitive activity</u> that involves <u>physical exertion</u> (uses energy and your muscles).
2) Sports have <u>rules</u> and <u>regulations</u> so people can play <u>correctly</u>, <u>safely</u> and <u>fairly</u>.
3) Each sport has a <u>National Governing Body</u> to <u>oversee</u> and <u>develop</u> the sport, e.g. the <u>Football Association</u> and <u>British Gymnastics</u>.

There are Many Different Sports

Team sports

In a <u>team sport</u>, a <u>group</u> of players <u>compete together</u> against an <u>opposing team</u>.

Individual sports

In an <u>individual sport</u>, a participant <u>competes</u> by <u>themselves</u> against <u>at least one opponent</u>.

EXAMPLES

ultimate frisbee

volleyball   rugby   cricket

water polo   ice hockey

EXAMPLES

archery   boxing   bowls

golf   swimming   diving

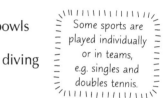

Some sports are played individually or in teams, e.g. singles and doubles tennis.

There are Benefits of Taking Part in Sport

Many people take part in sport for <u>fun</u>, but it can have other great <u>benefits</u> too.

Novelty size veggies ltd.

Now that's what I call shoplifting.

- **Improve fitness** — <u>regular physical activity</u> improves <u>components of fitness</u> (see p.32), such as aerobic endurance. Being <u>fit</u> makes <u>everyday tasks</u> like <u>climbing stairs</u> and <u>lifting shopping</u> much <u>easier</u>.

- **Meet new people** — sport involves interacting with <u>other people</u>, so it can be a great way to <u>make friends</u> and <u>talk to people</u> with a common interest.

- **Develop teamwork skills** — team sports encourage <u>cooperation</u> to <u>achieve a shared goal</u>.

- **Develop leadership skills** — <u>leading</u> a <u>team</u> gives <u>confidence</u> with <u>taking control</u> of situations.

- **Improve resilience** — <u>competitions</u> are <u>challenging</u>, can take you outside of your <u>comfort zone</u>, and will often involve <u>losing</u> to others. Competing in sport develops <u>self-confidence</u> to <u>overcome difficult situations</u> in other areas of life.

Sport — I'm incompete without you...

You'll know many, *many* more examples of sports. It's important to remember that a sport must be in a competitive environment, so swimming is only an example of a sport if you're competing against others.

Outdoor Activities

Outdoor activities are another great way of being active and learning some new skills.

Outdoor Activities are Adventurous

1) Outdoor activities are done outside in natural settings or specially-built recreation areas.
2) They are adventurous and can give you a chance to explore new places.
3) Many outdoor activities also involve taking risks. Safety equipment is often used for these activities, but this does not make the activity totally risk-free.
4) Here are some examples of outdoor activities:

Hiking — a long-distance walk across trails and footpaths in the countryside.

White water rafting — an activity that involves navigating through rough water in an inflatable raft.

Brace yourselves, it's a bit choppy ahead.

Abseiling — an activity that involves descending down a cliff face or climbing wall using a rope and harness.

High ropes course — a suspended obstacle course with ladders, nets, tightropes and zip lines.

Mountain biking — an activity with specialist bicycles that involves riding off-road on rough terrain.

Being Outdoors has Mental Health Benefits

Taking part in outdoor activities has the same physical and social benefits as sport, such as increasing your overall fitness and learning new skills. There are some great mental health benefits too.

- **Positive risk-taking** — outdoor activities such as rock climbing or rafting have some risk involved, which helps to develop your confidence and resilience.

As with sport, outdoor activities let you bond with people over shared experiences.

- **Improve self-confidence and self-esteem** — you feel a sense of achievement when you complete something challenging or risky, e.g. hiking to the top of a mountain or finishing a difficult mountain bike trail.

- **Time away from life stresses and devices** — being outdoors gets you away from normal life. This means you spend less time looking at electronic devices, such as a smartphone, which helps you reduce stress and appreciate nature.

OMG, just finished episode 5

Please go outside. Mum x

Did you hear about the monarch on the mountain? He was a hiking...

Taking part in outdoor activities can push you outside of your comfort zone and they are highly rewarding. Make sure you can remember examples of these activities and the benefits that they bring to participants.

Physical Fitness Activities

Here's another page on the types of physical activity you can do.

Physical Fitness Activities are also Popular

1) People do physical fitness activities to increase their fitness and physical health.
2) Popular activities include fitness classes, going to the gym and exercises in the home.

Fitness classes

A fitness class is a structured workout led by an instructor or trainer.
Here are examples of well-known fitness classes:

- Pilates — a low-impact workout focused on core strength.
- Zumba® — a high-energy dance workout inspired by Latin dancing.
- Water aerobics — low-impact exercises performed in water, often to music.

Gym exercises

A gym has lots of equipment that can be used to increase components of fitness, such as aerobic endurance, muscular endurance and strength. Examples include free weights, treadmills and cross-trainers.

Other fitness activities

Other ways to keep fit include going for a run, swimming and cycling. There are exercises you can do in the home, such as press-ups or sit-ups, and different stretches. Online exercise classes are also very popular.

There are More Benefits than Just Increased Fitness

Here are some other benefits in taking part in physical fitness activities:

- **Set fitness goals** — fitness goals, e.g. a target to run a marathon in under 4 hours, are motivating and highlight strengths and areas for improvement in your overall fitness.

- **Improve body composition** — exercise helps reduce body fat and increase muscle mass. A healthy weight reduces strain on the body and reduces risk of illnesses (see p.10).

- **Improved confidence** — exercise makes you feel good about yourself. You may be more outgoing if you develop a positive body image (see p.13).

- **Meet new people** — joining a fitness class or gym can help you make friends and meet new people in your local area.

All these benefits of exercise and I'm sitting around writing jokes...

There are a great number of benefits of taking part in sport and physical activity, and you'll have your own reasons for participating too. Take your time to jot down all the key benefits before you turn over the page.

Types of Provision

There are different ways that you can access sport and physical activity.

There are Three Types of Provision

1) To participate in many sports and activities, you need access to certain facilities (e.g. swimming pools, football pitches) and equipment (e.g. rackets, weights, balls).

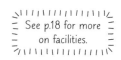
See p.18 for more on facilities.

2) There are three sectors that provide sport and physical activities:

public   **private**   **voluntary**

3) Each sector has its own aims and funding source, which means there are different levels of accessibility and quality of provision.

The Public Sector Includes School and Local Authority Provision

1) The public sector includes anything owned by the Government.
2) After-school sports clubs and fitness or swimming classes run by local authorities are examples of activities provided by the public sector.

Characteristics of public provision

- The aim is to make sport low-cost and accessible for all, so everyone has an opportunity to participate in exercise.
- Funding is provided by the Government using money from taxes.
- However, the standard and quality of provision varies due to limited funding.

Advantages and Disadvantages:

Advantages:
- A wide range of sports and activities are often available.
- Facilities are open to everyone in the community.
- Cheaper membership than private clubs or 'pay per visit' options.

Disadvantages:
- Limited range of equipment and facilities.
- Some equipment and facilities can be old or dated.
- Limited access to sports sector professionals, e.g. physiotherapists and personal trainers.
- Additional charges can apply to hire equipment.

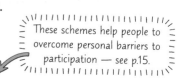
These schemes help people to overcome personal barriers to participation — see p.15.

There are also Government-led schemes to encourage participation:
- 'This Girl Can' — a campaign to inspire women of all ages to take part in exercise.
- 'Couch to 5K' — a popular running plan for beginners to get running in nine weeks.

Types of Provision

Private Provision **is about** Making a Profit

1) The <u>private sector</u> includes provision by <u>individuals</u> or <u>companies</u> that the Government <u>does not own</u>.
2) Examples include <u>private gyms</u>, such as <u>David Lloyd gyms</u>, and classes with <u>personal trainers</u>.

Characteristics of private provision

- The aim is to make a <u>profit</u>.
- <u>Funding</u> is provided by <u>investors</u>, and participants usually pay a <u>membership fee</u> to join.
- <u>Less accessible</u> than public provision due to <u>higher fees</u>.
- <u>High-quality provision</u>, including <u>modern</u> facilities and equipment.

Advantages and Disadvantages:

Advantages:
- A <u>wide range</u> of sports and activities are often available.
- <u>Additional equipment</u> and <u>facilities</u> are offered, e.g. <u>refreshments</u> and <u>crèche facilities</u> (child care).
- Access to <u>sports sector professionals</u> is often included as part of membership.

Disadvantages:
- It is <u>more expensive</u> to join than public provision.
- Facilities are only available in areas where there is <u>demand</u>.

Voluntary Provision **is Run by** Volunteers

1) The <u>voluntary sector</u> provides activities by <u>volunteers</u> who share a <u>common interest</u> in a sport or physical activity.
2) <u>Most amateur clubs</u> are in the voluntary sector, such as local <u>athletics</u> and <u>hockey clubs</u>.

Characteristics of voluntary provision

- The aim is <u>not</u> to make a <u>profit</u>. Volunteers <u>give up their own time</u> to <u>encourage</u> local people to <u>participate</u> in physical activity.
- <u>Funding</u> is <u>raised</u> through <u>sponsorship</u> from <u>local businesses</u> or <u>grants</u>. Participants <u>pay</u> to <u>cover match fees</u> and <u>costs</u> of <u>facilities</u> and <u>equipment</u>.
- Facilities are usually <u>hired</u> from the <u>public sector</u>, so the <u>quality of provision</u> and <u>accessibility</u> is the <u>same</u> as the public sector.

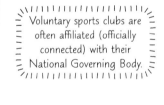
Voluntary sports clubs are often affiliated (officially connected) with their National Governing Body.

Advantages and Disadvantages:

Advantages:
- Opportunities to <u>volunteer</u> with <u>running</u> or <u>coaching</u> of clubs.
- Other advantages are the <u>same as public provision</u>.

Disadvantages:
- Relies on <u>volunteers</u> to operate and <u>money</u> from <u>sponsorship</u> and <u>fundraising</u>.
- Other disadvantages are the <u>same as public provision</u>.

[Sponsor this tip today!]
Private sector companies have fancier facilities and other benefits, but you'll have to pay more to use them. For many people, public and voluntary provision is much more accessible due to the lower fees involved.

Participants of Different Ages

There are different types of participants in sport and recommended government guidelines for physical activity.

Participants in Sport have Different Needs

1) Physical activity has physical, social and mental health benefits.
2) Activities should be planned around the needs of the participant.
3) Their needs depend on many factors, such as age, current fitness and whether they have any disabilities or long-term health conditions.

Your participation in sport varies as you get older — there are four age groups to learn...

Children are Active and Learn Many Skills

The UK Chief Medical Officers' Physical Activity Guidelines suggest that children and adolescents:

- do an average of at least 60 minutes of moderate or vigorous activity per day across the week.
- take part in a variety of activities to develop movement skills and strengthen muscles and bones.
- reduce the time spent sitting or lying down and break up long periods of inactivity (not moving).

Children may get their daily exercise from walking to school, taking part in playground activities or after-school sports such as football, tennis and gymnastics.

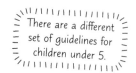

There are a different set of guidelines for children under 5.

Primary School children (5-11 years)

1) Primary school children should be encouraged to do lots of physical activity.
2) They take part in PE lessons and have breaks during the school day for exercise.
3) Making sport fun is important so they are interested and want to do more in the future.

improve fitness

Physical needs

improve skills and coordination

boost immunity to prevent illness

have fun

Social needs

develop teamwork and leadership skills

support learning, e.g. problem-solving

Mental needs

increase confidence and self-esteem

Adolescents (12-17 years)

1) Adolescents are physically changing from being a child into an adult.
2) Physical activity is important to help support the body as it grows and develops.
3) Exercise also has useful mental benefits to cope with anxious thoughts and stress from exams.

improve fitness

Physical needs

improve body composition

better sleep

develop teamwork and leadership skills

Social needs

make new friends

meet new people

improve mood

Mental needs

decrease stress

decrease risk of depression

Participants of Different Ages

Adults **have to Balance Work** and **Exercise**

The UK Chief Medical Officers' Physical Activity
Guidelines suggest that adults and older adults:

> It's a strengthening exercise, honest.

- do at least 150 minutes of moderate activity or 75 minutes of vigorous activity a week.
- do strengthening activities to work all major muscle groups at least twice a week.
- reduce time spent sitting or lying down and break up long periods of inactivity (not moving).
- do balancing exercises twice a week to reduce chance of frailty and falls (older adults only).

Adults may take part in sport or do physical fitness activities such as yoga and water aerobics.
Even chores such as vacuuming and dusting are useful to reduce inactivity.

Adults (18-49 years)

1) Many adults have a job or a family to support, so they have less time for exercise.
2) Physical activity can help to reduce stress from work and encourage a good
   work-life balance (spending a healthy time between working and leisure).

improve body composition · improve fitness

Physical needs

reduce symptoms of long-term health issues · better sleep

meet new people

Social needs

make new friends

decrease stress

Mental needs

improve work-life balance · decrease risk of depression

Older adults (50+ years)

1) Retired adults may have more spare time to take part in physical activity.
2) Older adults have an increased risk of long-term health conditions.
   Physical activity can decrease this risk by improving bone strength and heart health.
3) Older adults are more likely to live by themselves, so physical activity
   allows them to socialise and avoid loneliness.

improve fitness

Physical needs

reduce symptoms of long-term health issues · better sleep

decrease loneliness

Social needs

make new friends

decrease stress

Mental needs

decrease risk of depression

Bread has lots of physical kneads...

There is overlap between each group's needs, but there are key differences, e.g. children have a particular
need for developing teamwork skills, whereas for older adults avoiding loneliness may be a greater need.

Disabilities and Long-Term Health Conditions

Sport should be <u>inclusive</u> for everyone, which can require <u>adapting</u> how a sport is played.

Sports can be Adapted for Disabilities

1) There are a <u>wide range</u> of <u>disabilities</u>. Many are <u>non-visible</u> (a condition that is <u>not obvious</u>).

2) Some disabilities <u>don't prevent</u> people <u>participating</u> in sport or physical activities <u>alongside non-disabled participants</u>.

3) However, some sports have been <u>adapted</u>, or <u>created</u>, so that they're <u>more accessible</u>, e.g:

wheelchair basketball — adapted from <u>basketball</u>, for people with <u>physical impairments</u>.

goalball — a <u>team sport</u> where players must <u>remain silent</u> and aim to throw a <u>ball with bells inside</u> towards an opponent's <u>goal</u>.

All participants wear eye coverings, so goalball can be played with fully sighted people and people with visual impairments.

boccia — a <u>team</u> or <u>individual sport</u> for people with <u>physical impairments</u>, where players <u>throw</u>, <u>kick</u> or <u>roll</u> leather balls towards a <u>white target ball</u>.

4) <u>Disabled adults</u> should follow the <u>same guidelines</u> for physical activity as <u>non-disabled adults</u> (see p.9). <u>Disabled children</u> should aim for at least <u>20 minutes</u> of <u>moderate</u> or <u>vigorous</u> activity a <u>day</u>.

5) However, doing the <u>recommended</u> activity can be <u>difficult</u> where there are a <u>lack of facilities</u> or <u>specialist equipment</u>. This means there is <u>less opportunity</u> for them to <u>participate</u> in sport.

Exercise is Beneficial if you have a Long-Term Health Condition

1) Many people live with <u>long-term health conditions</u>, including:

Coronary heart disease

- Coronary heart disease is when the <u>arteries</u> that supply blood to the heart get <u>blocked</u> by <u>layers of fatty material building up</u>.
- Symptoms include <u>chest pain</u> and <u>dizziness</u> and the condition can lead to <u>heart attacks</u>.

Type-2 diabetes

- Type-2 diabetes occurs when the body <u>doesn't respond</u> properly to a hormone called <u>insulin</u>. This can cause <u>blood sugar levels</u> to <u>rise</u> to dangerous levels.
- Symptoms include feeling <u>thirsty</u>, frequent <u>urination</u>, <u>fatigue</u> and <u>weight loss</u>.

Asthma

- Asthma is a <u>lung condition</u> where the airways become <u>narrow</u> and <u>swollen</u>, which can make it <u>difficult</u> to <u>breathe</u>.
- Symptoms include <u>coughing</u>, <u>wheezing</u>, <u>chest tightness</u> and <u>breathlessness</u>.

High blood pressure

- <u>High blood pressure</u> puts strain on your <u>blood vessels</u> and other <u>organs</u>.
- Most people have <u>no symptoms</u>, but have an <u>increased risk</u> of <u>strokes</u> and <u>heart attacks</u>.

2) People with long-term health conditions may <u>believe</u> physical activity is <u>dangerous</u>, but <u>generally</u> it is <u>safe</u> and can <u>reduce</u> some of the <u>symptoms</u>.

3) It is <u>best</u> if they start at a level that <u>feels right for them</u> and gradually <u>build up</u> activity.

4) It is sensible to get <u>medical advice</u> if someone <u>experiences worsening symptoms</u>.

Physical activity can also reduce the risk of <u>developing</u> some long-term health conditions.

Participation — you have to be in it to win it...

Unfortunately, a disability or health condition can limit the physical activity you can do. But exercise has lots of benefits, so these groups of people should aim to participate in activities that are suitable for them.

Barriers to Participation

Many different factors can prevent someone participating in sport or physical activities.
The next three pages cover all of these barriers.

Barriers Get in the Way of Participating in Sport and Physical Activity

A barrier is something that stops people from participating in regular sport and physical activity.
There are many barriers that people may have to overcome to participate.

The five main categories are cost, access, time, cultural barriers and personal barriers.

Cost

There are various costs involved in sport. People may have little money to spend on sport after
essentials such as bills and food. Some sports are very expensive, such as skiing or horse riding.

Clothing

Some sports require specialist clothing, such as karate uniforms, which can be expensive.

Equipment

Equipment is required to play most sports, e.g. golf clubs
or snowboards. This equipment can also be expensive.

Transport

It costs money to run a car or to use public transport to get to a facility.

Access

Where you live affects the types of sport that are available to you.

Location

The location of some sports can be too far away. For example, it is difficult to
go sailing if you live far from the sea or a lake, or hiking if you live in a big city.

Transport

If you do not have a car and there are poor public transport
links and cycling routes, some facilities may not be accessible.

Resources

Sports equipment, like canoes or bikes, must be stored or transported. Facilities may not be able
to afford to buy or have room to store equipment, and it might be impractical to bring your own.

Types of sport

Some sports require specialist facilities, like ski slopes, ice rinks and velodromes (track cycling).
You can't easily take part in these sports if you live in an area without these facilities.

Barriers to Participation

Time

People can have a <u>lack of time</u> to take part in physical activity because of other <u>commitments</u>.

Family

Many adults have a <u>family</u> to look after and <u>spend time</u> with. <u>Parents</u> may not have the <u>time</u> and <u>energy</u> for physical activity whilst taking care of their <u>baby</u> or <u>young child</u>.

School

Children must attend <u>school</u>, which takes up a lot of time on <u>weekdays</u>. Teenagers <u>study</u> and <u>prepare for exams</u> outside of school hours too.

Work

<u>Working adults</u> can only take part in sport or physical activity <u>outside</u> of their <u>working hours</u>. If they work <u>shifts</u> or <u>irregular hours</u>, it can be hard to join clubs that meet in <u>evenings</u> or the <u>weekend</u>.

Cultural Barriers

<u>Religious beliefs</u>, <u>ethnicity</u> and <u>culture</u> all influence the physical activity you do. People can be treated <u>differently</u> because of their <u>background</u>.

Social norms

A <u>social norm</u> is an 'acceptable' behaviour. In sport, this can include the clothing that people <u>expect</u> you to wear. This can be a barrier for people with <u>religious beliefs</u>. E.g. many <u>Muslim women</u> keep their bodies <u>covered up</u>, so wear <u>full-body swimsuits</u> for swimming. However, these swimsuits are not <u>easily available</u> and may be seen as <u>unconventional</u>, which creates a <u>barrier to participation</u>.

Single-sex sport

Some people only take part in sport with people of the <u>same sex</u> because of <u>religious beliefs</u>. There are also <u>outdated attitudes</u> towards <u>certain sports</u> being for '<u>women</u>' or '<u>men</u>' only.

Role models

A <u>role model</u> is someone <u>inspirational</u> who you <u>look up to</u>.

A <u>lack</u> of role models and <u>media coverage</u> of <u>professional sportspeople</u> from your <u>background</u> will not <u>motivate</u> you to try sport.

<u>Ethnic minorities</u> (along with <u>women</u> and the <u>elderly</u>) often have fewer role models in sport.

It's called fashion, darling.

Barriers to Participation

Personal Barriers

Some personal barriers are related to self-confidence and family influence.

Body image

Body image is how we feel about our physical appearance.

Some people may not feel confident with their appearance, which can make them feel self-conscious in tight-fitting clothing, e.g. leotards or swimsuits.

Self-confidence

Someone with low confidence may not feel able to start a new sport or may want to stop competing in a sport. This could be because of a negative experience or a poor series of results, e.g. losing football games.

Parental influence

A parent or guardian can influence the physical activity of their child.

Children may be pressured to take part in a sport, or not take part in sport at all if their carer isn't very active or has a negative attitude to sport.

Limited previous participation

It is difficult to try a new sport when you lack the confidence and knowledge of the rules and there are other participants with much more experience.

You may have tried sports in the past and not enjoyed them, so are put off from trying other sports and physical activities.

Some personal barriers are related to health reasons.

Low fitness levels

Low fitness means that simple tasks such as walking or lifting things can make you out of breath. Unfit people may feel embarrassed about taking part in sport in case it is too challenging for them.

Extended time off

It takes time to recover from injuries and it is easy to lose fitness and confidence in your abilities during this time. After recovery, it can be worrying to take part in activity with a risk of re-injury.

Existing health conditions

People with long-term health conditions may fear that exercise may make their condition worse, so may stop doing physical activity altogether.

Step 1: Role model. Step 2: Run down the hill and collect it...

Loads of barriers were thrown at you there, but don't be put off. Try covering up each of the five categories of barriers and write down as much as you can remember. Then repeat until you've remembered it all.

Overcoming Barriers

Now for a few pages on some of the solutions that help people overcome the barriers to participation.

Removing Barriers Helps to Increase Participation

Cost

Discounts — clubs can offer reduced prices for classes or reduced membership fees for groups such as students, the elderly or unemployed people who may have less money to spend on sport.

Free parking — leisure centres often offer free parking, which reduces the overall cost of participating in classes.

Hiring equipment — equipment can be expensive, so facilities may allow people to hire equipment at a reasonable cost. This is useful for trying a new sport because you can hire equipment first and buy your own later.

Access

Public transport discounts — leisure clubs may run promotions where members get free travel to facilities. Groups such as the elderly and disabled people are entitled to free off-peak bus travel.

Cycle hire — many urban areas have cycle lanes. Hiring a bike can be a more affordable, efficient and healthy way to access facilities in these areas.

Free parking can also be described as an access solution too.

Taster days — free sessions encourage people to try their local facilities and 'try before they buy'. They can experience a sport or class before they have to pay anything.

Staff training — increasing awareness of the different types of participant (see p.8-10) can help staff meet their participants' needs.

Variety — facilities may offer a wide range of sports and physical activities or introduce new classes to make sure there is something for everyone.

Access ramps — facilities may build ramps for wheelchair users as an alternative to stairs.

Assistive technology

Assistive technology is equipment or systems that help those with disabilities and the elderly. This is important so that everyone has the same access to facilities and information, e.g.

- Pool hoists — a chair that helps lower disabled swimmers into the water.
- Braille — a system of raised dots on leaflets and signs that assists visually impaired people.
- Hearing (induction) loops — a sound system that assists wearers of hearing aids.

Overcoming Barriers

Time

Crèche facilities — a crèche is a place where children can be cared for, which can give parents time to participate in physical activity, e.g. attend a yoga class.

Extended opening hours — facilities which open earlier or later in the day allow people who work full time more opportunity to access them. Some gyms are open 24 hours a day.

Cultural Barriers

Women-only sessions — introducing women-only sessions with all-female staff benefits women who do single-sex sport due to religious beliefs. It may also make some women feel more comfortable as some environments can be very male-dominated.

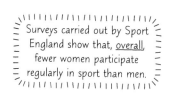

Surveys carried out by Sport England show that, overall, fewer women participate regularly in sport than men.

Staff diversity — a more diverse workforce may attract a more diverse community to use a facility, and may provide role models for minorities.

Staff training — an awareness of religious and cultural beliefs will allow staff to be more considerate of participants' needs.

Personal Barriers

Private changing rooms — people may be more comfortable changing in private cubicles instead of open-plan changing rooms, because of worries over body image or for religious reasons.

Relaxed clothing requirements — allowing people to wear looser or full-length clothing may also help people overcome issues concerning body image.

Variety of body shapes — using images of people of different body sizes in branding or when promoting a facility can make people feel more welcome.

Parent and child sessions — these sessions get the child and parent both active, which can help the child to develop a positive relationship with sport from an early age.

Campaigns — there are many national campaigns that promote physical activity and encourage healthy habits, such as the Daily Mile or Change4Life.

Hurdlers have to overcome all sorts of barriers...

That's all of the solutions to the barriers to participation that you need to know. Think about your own experiences and the barriers you faced, and which solutions could have helped overcome those barriers.

Component 1 — A4: Addressing Barriers to Participation

Sports Clothing and Equipment

Clothing and equipment are essential for sport — try ice hockey without an ice rink or a pair of ice skates...

Clothing and Footwear are Adapted for Each Sport

Sports clothing and footwear help participants to perform at their best.

Clothing

Performance clothing — clothing that is adapted to improve performance, e.g. sweat-wicking football shirts or stretchy skinsuits (see p.19).

Training clothing — clothing used in training drills and practice sessions. For example, bibs are used to quickly divide players into teams and GPS vests help with performance analysis (see p.21).

Waterproof clothing — clothing that resists water, which is essential to keep you dry in poor weather during outdoor activities such as hiking, cycling or kayaking.

Footwear

1) Good footwear is supportive and provides grip to stop participants from slipping over.
2) The type of footwear depends on the surface and activity:
   - Trainers are general-purpose and cushioned to prevent blisters whilst running.
   - Studded boots are used in some team sports played on grass or artificial turf, e.g. rugby.
   - Spiked shoes are used in track events and activities on rough terrain, e.g. cross-country running.

See p.19 for more on sport-specific footwear.

 EXAMPLES

tight-fit shorts
vest
spiked shoes

Sprinter

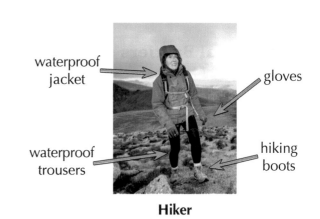

waterproof jacket
gloves
waterproof trousers
hiking boots

Hiker

Sport-Specific Equipment is Essential for Sport

Each sport or physical activity requires sport-specific equipment. There are four categories, as shown below.

- **Travel equipment** — equipment for activities that involve movement, e.g. kayaks, skateboards, bicycles and skis.
- **Participation equipment** — essential equipment needed to participate, e.g. rugby balls, tennis rackets, golf clubs and relay batons.
- **Fitness training equipment** — equipment to improve fitness, e.g. dumbbells, resistance bands, treadmills and kettlebells.
- **Scoring equipment** — equipment needed for scoring, e.g. goal posts, basketball hoops, football nets and archery targets.

Don't confuse travel equipment with things like cars and buses for getting to a facility.

Sports Clothing and Equipment

Equipment is used for Protection and Safety

Protective and safety equipment is important to prevent injury to participants.

Protective Equipment

Most sports have protective equipment. It is often a rule to wear it, but it can be optional.
Personal protective equipment (PPE) protects against impact to areas of the body, e.g:

- Head — helmet (cycling), scrum hat (rugby), face mask (baseball)
- Mouth — gumshield/mouth guard (rugby, hockey, boxing)
- Eyes — goggles (horse racing, cycling, squash)
- Body — chest protector (ice hockey), shoulder pads (American football)
- Arms — elbow pads (rollerblading)
- Legs/Groin — leg pads (cricket), box/cup (cricket — male only), shin pads (football)

Safety Equipment

1) Flotation devices such as life jackets keep the wearer afloat in bodies of water — vital for water-based outdoor activities where there is a risk of drowning.

2) Floats and pool noodles (woggles) also help those learning to swim.

3) Other safety equipment includes crash mats to cushion landings or falls (e.g. in trampolining or judo) and harnesses (e.g. in rock climbing).

Let me hold on to you.

First Aid Equipment is Necessary to Treat Injuries

I'm not that kind of boy ant.

Injuries in sport are common, even when protective and safety equipment is used.
First aid equipment should always be available to quickly deal with any injury.

First Aid Equipment

- Ice packs reduce swelling from strains and sprains.
- Bandages control bleeding, reduce swelling and provide support to limbs and joints. They also reduce the risk of a wound becoming infected.
- Defibrillators are life-saving devices that treat someone in cardiac arrest. They deliver an electrical current to restore a normal heartbeat.

Disability Sports may include Modified Equipment

1) Disability sports include adapted sports and new sports designed for people with disabilities.

2) These sports may use modified sport-specific equipment, e.g. javelins and shots may be lighter than usual, and lower nets are used in sports such as sitting volleyball.

3) Other sports have specifically designed equipment — e.g. in boccia, ramps help people with physical impairments, and tactile (touch) boards allow people with no vision to play.

4) Runners with visual impairments may be tethered to a sighted guide who gives verbal directions.

5) There are also many wheelchair sports, such as wheelchair tennis and wheelchair basketball — each sport uses an adapted wheelchair that is specifically designed for that sport.

There's more on the technology used in disability sports on p.20.

Sports Clothing and Equipment

Officials use Equipment to Manage the Sport

1) Officials are people such as referees and umpires that manage the rules of a sport.

2) They need specific equipment during competition to score, time-keep, communicate and make decisions.

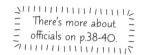
There's more about officials on p.38-40.

3) Examples include:

- Football referees use a whistle, a watch, an earpiece, disciplinary cards, etc.

- Field event judges use measuring tapes or electronic measuring systems to record the position of a thrown object.

- Track event judges use a starting pistol and stopwatch.

4) Officials may also rely on other technology, such as computers and video-assisted decision-making systems — see p.20.

Wearable Equipment is used for Performance Analysis

1) Performance analysis equipment is technology that records a participant's performance, which gives useful data on their overall fitness and how hard they were working at different times.

2) For example, wearable equipment like smartwatches, heart rate monitors and fitness trackers have sensors that records things like steps, heart rate and calories burned during physical activity.

3) Smartphone apps can also track various performance data, such as mapping a cycling route using GPS (Global Positioning System).

4) There is other performance analysis equipment that is more commonly used to coach high-level athletes — see p.21.

Facilities are Equally as Important as Sports Equipment

1) Facilities are purpose-built places for people to take part in sport and physical activity.

2) There are indoor and outdoor facilities. Some examples of facilities are shown in the tables below.

Indoor Facility	Example sports / activities
Sports hall	Basketball, badminton
Gym	Skipping, weight training
Swimming pool	Water aerobics, diving
Ice rink	Figure skating, ice hockey

Outdoor Facility	Example sports / activities
Grass pitch	Rugby, football
Artificial pitch	Hockey, lacrosse
Artificial ski slope	Skiing, snowboarding
Athletics track	Sprinting, distance running

3) There are benefits of modern facilities for performers — see p.21.

Right, time to equip my keyboard to write a quip here...

Try this task — think of two sports and list all of the clothing and equipment you need to take part in them. Also consider the different roles in the sport, e.g. goalkeepers need different equipment to outfield players.

Technology in Sport

Innovations in <u>technology</u> have led to <u>improvements</u> in <u>sports clothing</u> and <u>equipment</u>, as well as the development of <u>devices</u> and <u>apps</u>. Technology can <u>benefit</u> participants, officials and spectators of sport.

Clothing can be Aerodynamic or Regulate Temperature

1) Different <u>materials</u> have different <u>properties</u>, such as <u>durability</u> and <u>flexibility</u>.
2) This makes some materials <u>better suited</u> for <u>use in particular sports</u> than others.
3) Materials can be <u>natural</u>, e.g. <u>cotton</u>, or <u>synthetic</u> (man-made), e.g. <u>nylon</u>.

Improved aerodynamics

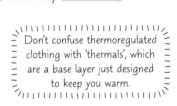

- <u>Synthetic materials</u>, such as <u>spandex</u>, are used for <u>aerodynamic clothing</u>, such as <u>skinsuits</u> for <u>track cycling</u>.
- These clothes are <u>tight-fitting</u>, <u>stretchy</u> and <u>comfortable</u>.
- They are designed to reduce the <u>drag force</u> from the <u>air</u>, which can <u>slow a participant down</u>.
- This helps performers travel <u>more efficiently</u> at <u>high speed</u>, and gain small <u>time advantages</u>.

Improved thermoregulation

- <u>Fine wool</u> or <u>synthetic materials</u>, such as <u>polyester</u>, are used in <u>base layer</u> clothing (a <u>thin-fit</u> layer worn close to the <u>skin</u>), which helps to <u>heat or cool</u> the body <u>effectively</u>.
- For example, <u>footballers</u> may wear a <u>base layer</u> to <u>trap heat</u> and keep them <u>warm</u> but also <u>remove sweat</u> to keep them <u>dry</u>.
- This is a <u>more comfortable</u> experience — being <u>cold</u> and <u>sweaty</u> is <u>unpleasant</u>, and can distract you from performing well.

Don't confuse thermoregulated clothing with 'thermals', which are a base layer just designed to keep you warm.

Footwear is all about Grip and Stability

New <u>materials</u> and <u>designs</u> in footwear can also provide a <u>benefit</u> to participants.

Improved grip

- Footwear with <u>strong grip</u> gives better <u>stability</u> and <u>quicker acceleration</u>. There is <u>less chance</u> of a participant <u>slipping</u> and <u>injuring themselves</u>.
- <u>Spiked shoes</u> are popular — they are <u>lighter</u> and <u>less cushioned</u> than trainers (to improve speed) and the <u>sharpened metal</u> or <u>ceramic</u> 'spikes' on the sole provide <u>stronger grip</u>.
- Spiked shoes can be <u>different</u> in each <u>sport</u>, for example:

    - <u>Sprinters</u> have spikes at the <u>front</u> of the shoe as they <u>run on their toes</u>.
    - <u>Cross-country runners</u> run <u>more flat-footed</u>, so may have shoes with <u>fewer</u>, <u>longer</u> spikes and <u>more cushioning</u> at the <u>heel</u>.

There can even be different footwear in the same sport, e.g. batters and bowlers in cricket wear different shoes.

Improved rebound

- <u>Rebound</u> is the amount of <u>spring</u> provided by a shoe.
- <u>Improved rebound</u> allows participants to <u>jump higher</u> or <u>further</u>, which is important for sports such as <u>basketball</u> and <u>netball</u>, where participants are constantly <u>jumping</u>.
- It also helps to <u>reduce</u> the risk of <u>impact injuries</u>.

Technology in Sport

Composite Materials Improve Safety and Performance

1) Equipment can be made lighter and stronger by using new or composite materials. Composite materials are made by combining materials with different properties.

2) The materials and design of sport-specific and safety equipment is constantly reviewed and improved with the aim of making participants perform better and have more protection.

	Sport-specific equipment	Protective/safety equipment
Lighter materials	Participants exert less energy to use lighter equipment, e.g. tennis rackets made of carbon fibre instead of wood. These rackets are easier to move and players can generate more speed with their shots.	Lighter equipment is more comfortable and doesn't reduce performance as much, e.g. mouthguards can be moulded to fit a participant's mouth. These obstruct breathing less and still absorb shock.
Stronger materials	More robust equipment, e.g. fibreglass kayaks, lasts for a longer time, meaning you won't need to replace it as often.	Stronger equipment provides more protection to participants, e.g. titanium cricket helmets.
Improved design	The shape of equipment can be made more aerodynamic, e.g. a golf driver. This reduces drag on the swing, which means more power and distance on the golf ball.	The shape of equipment can be made more aerodynamic, e.g. cycling helmets. This gives marginal gains (small improvements) to a participant, but still provides good protection.

Assistive Technology includes Prosthetics and Sports Wheelchairs

Assistive technology supports people with disabilities. Here are some examples:

- Prosthetics (artificial body parts), such as running blades, allow athletes with limb differences to compete in running and track events.
- Sports wheelchairs are modified, lighter wheelchairs with larger, angled (cambered) wheels. They can make sharper turns and are more stable. There are other modifications depending on the sport, e.g. rugby wheelchairs have large, defensive wings.
- Sound devices in equipment help people with visual impairments, e.g. to locate the ball in goalball.
- Assistive listening devices can amplify sound to help people with hearing impairments.

Technology Helps Officials make Correct Decisions

Many sports make use of technology during matches to help referees and umpires. These systems aim to make the sport fairer, which can benefit both the spectators and participants.

- Hawk-Eye (tennis) — Hawk-Eye uses six cameras to track and show the path of the ball. It's used so that players can challenge decisions on whether shots are in or out.
- Decision Review System (cricket) — players can challenge an umpire's decision and have it reviewed by the third umpire, who uses various bits of technology to decide whether the on-field umpire was correct or not. 'Owzaaaat?!
- Television Match Official (rugby union) — the TMO is an extra official who watches video replays.
- Video Assistant Referee (football) — the VAR watches the match on various screens and can watch slow-motion replays. They advise the on-field referee of any 'clear and obvious' errors they have made which resulted in a goal or a player being sent off (red card).

Component 1 — B2: Benefits of Technology in Sport

Technology in Sport

Performance Analysis is Useful for Coaching

1) Performance analysis identifies strengths and weaknesses of an athlete's performance, which can support coaches when planning future strategies, tactics and training sessions.
2) It can compare the performance of one athlete against the performance of another.
3) Or coaches may use performance analysis to set targets for an athlete.

Action cameras

Action cameras are designed to take snapshots of a fast-moving subject.

For example, an action camera could capture a diver in mid-dive to check their arms are in the correct position.

Apps

Performance analysis apps have many features such as playing back video in slow motion, adding narration or watching two videos at the same time.

GPS trackers

GPS is a system which uses signals from satellites to track the distance and speed of a subject over time.

- GPS vests can provide a 'heat map' to show the ground a performer covers in a match.
- Running watches with GPS can record split times in races such as marathons.

Sensors

Sensors can be attached to equipment or clothing. E.g. smart tennis rackets use vibrations to give feedback about where on the racket contact is made.

Modern Facilities are Usable in All Weathers and are Safer

New technology can also improve the facilities that participants train in.

Replicate other environments

- Facilities can recreate the same conditions as a competition. Participants benefit because they know what to expect and can practise effectively.
- For example, beach volleyball players can use indoor sand courts that replicate real beaches, and white-water rafters can use man-made facilities that replicate natural rivers.

Usable in all weathers

- Artificial pitches, e.g. MUGAs (multi-use games areas), are made of artificial turf or rubber.
- Sport can be played all year round and in poor weather because the pitch doesn't freeze or flood.
- These pitches have low upkeep as you don't need to cut grass or repaint any lines.

Reduce risk of injury

4G is the '4th generation' of technology used for artificial pitches. 2G, 3G, 5G and 6G pitches also exist.

- Materials for surfaces are chosen to reduce injuries.
- For example, 4G pitches are often cushioned to reduce impact injuries and gymnastics floors are sprung to absorb the shock of landing.

Thought I'd test out these new aerodynamic tip boxes...

Equipment is constantly evolving as manufacturers tinker with things like materials, style and quality. Wooden tennis rackets, for example, were common but rackets are now made with materials like graphite.

Limitations of Technology

Technology can be very useful, but it does have <u>limitations</u> and <u>negative effects</u> too.

Unequal Access gives Unfair Advantages

1) Participants can have an <u>unfair advantage</u> if they have greater <u>access</u> to <u>technology</u> over their <u>competitors</u>. E.g. a <u>sprinter</u> with the latest pair of <u>spiked shoes</u> will <u>have an advantage</u> over someone wearing <u>regular trainers</u>.

2) New technology can be <u>expensive</u> (see below), which means it is usually more <u>common</u> in <u>wealthy countries</u> that can afford it.

3) Even <u>within</u> the same <u>country</u>, some people will be <u>prevented</u> from accessing <u>facilities</u> or <u>training programmes</u> using <u>new technology</u> because of the <u>cost</u> or <u>location</u>.

New Technology can Cost a Lot of Money

1) Technology can be very <u>expensive</u>, preventing many <u>sports clubs</u> and <u>participants</u> from taking advantage of it.

2) There is the <u>initial cost</u> of <u>buying equipment</u> and the cost of <u>further maintenance</u> if it becomes <u>faulty</u>.

3) <u>Private clubs</u> can usually <u>afford</u> more <u>advanced equipment</u> compared to <u>facilities</u> in the <u>public sector</u>.

4) <u>Professional sports teams</u> with <u>more money</u> than other teams can also <u>invest</u> in <u>new technology</u>. For example, <u>richer countries</u> (like the <u>UK</u>) can build <u>better-performing</u> track cycles than other countries, which gives them a significant <u>advantage</u> in <u>international events</u>.

Reviewing Performance Data takes Time

1) <u>Time</u> can be a <u>limitation</u> when using <u>performance analysis equipment</u>.

2) <u>Setting up</u> and <u>using</u> the technology can take a long time, e.g. fitting a team with <u>GPS vests</u>.

3) Then a coach must <u>review</u> and <u>compile</u> the <u>data</u> and give <u>feedback</u> to each participant. For <u>team sports</u> with lots of participants, <u>individual feedback</u> is <u>time-consuming</u> — this means the coach may have <u>less time</u> to <u>run</u> training sessions.

Some Technology requires an Expert to Use

1) Most '<u>smart technology</u>' relies on the <u>Internet</u>, which isn't easy to <u>access</u> in <u>remote areas</u>.

2) Some <u>apps</u> can have lots of <u>features</u>, making them <u>complicated</u> and <u>difficult</u> to use.

3) <u>Performance analysis equipment</u> needs a <u>specialist</u> who knows how to <u>use the equipment</u> correctly and <u>interpret the data</u> accurately.

Data is Not Always Accurate

1) Technology is <u>not perfect</u>, which means it can <u>provide inaccurate data</u>.

2) For example, a <u>fitness tracker</u> may <u>record too many steps</u>, which can give the <u>wrong</u> impression about a participant's <u>fitness</u>.

Seems a tad inaccurate...

3000 steps

I'm trying to tech this all in, but I only have limited capacity...

If you're struggling to remember all these limitations, the word <u>ACTUAL</u> is a good memory aid — <u>A</u>ccess, <u>C</u>ost, <u>T</u>ime, <u>U</u>sability and <u>A</u>ccuracy are all <u>L</u>imitations of technology in sport.

Body Systems

It's important to understand how the body systems work and how they respond to exercise.

The Cardiorespiratory System Gets Oxygenated Blood to the Muscles

Cardiovascular System

1) The cardiovascular (circulatory) system moves blood around the body.
2) It is made up of the heart, blood vessels and blood.

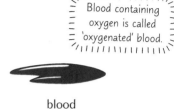

blood vessels   the heart   blood

Blood containing oxygen is called 'oxygenated' blood.

Respiratory System

1) The respiratory system moves air into and out of the body.
2) It is made up of the nose, mouth, trachea (windpipe), lungs and other airways.
3) The diaphragm and intercostal muscles are respiratory muscles (see p.85) which assist in breathing.

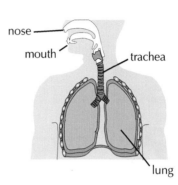

nose — mouth — trachea — lung

1) The cardiovascular system and respiratory system make up the cardiorespiratory system.
2) It allows us to breathe in air to the lungs.
3) Oxygen (from the air) passes from the lungs into the blood and is transported around the body.
4) Our muscles use oxygen to release energy and contract (work).
5) The system also allows us to remove carbon dioxide (a waste product) from the body.
6) It is transported in the blood to the lungs where it is breathed out.

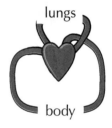

lungs — body

The Musculoskeletal System allows Movement

1) The skeletal system (skeleton) and the muscular system make up the musculoskeletal system.
2) Muscles connect to the skeleton and allow movement of the body.
3) These muscles contract and pull on bones to make us move.
4) Bones move at joints. A joint is where two or more bones meet. Most joints in our bodies are synovial joints:

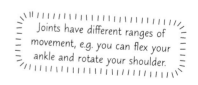

Joints have different ranges of movement, e.g. you can flex your ankle and rotate your shoulder.

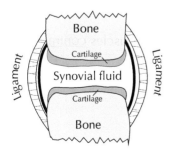

Bone — Cartilage — Synovial fluid — Cartilage — Bone — Ligament — Ligament

- Synovial fluid lubricates (or 'oils') the joint, allowing it to move more easily.

- The ends of bones are covered with cartilage, which acts as a shock absorber (cushion) to prevent damage during joint movement.

Body Systems

Learn the Names of These Muscle Groups

1) Each muscle in the body has a specific function, for example:

- the biceps are used to close (flex) the elbow joint.

- the quadriceps are used to open (extend) the knee joint.

- the hip flexors are a group of muscles in the lower back, hips, groin and thigh that close (flex) the hip joint.

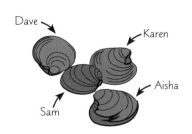

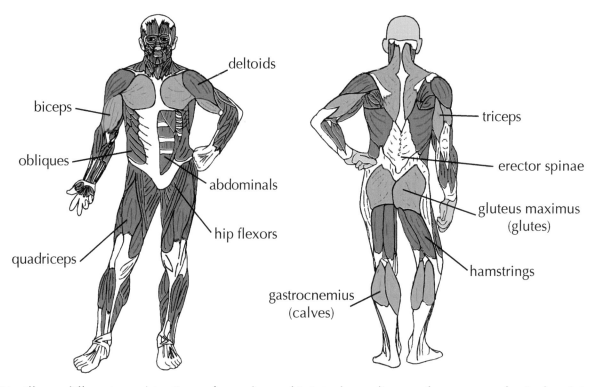

2) You'll use different combinations of muscles and joints depending on the sport or physical activity.
3) It's important to stretch the muscles in a warm-up to match the activity you're about to do (see p.29).

Connective Tissue Joins Muscles and Bones

Ligaments and tendons are types of connective tissue that are also part of the musculoskeletal system:

- Ligaments — connect bones together to restrict how much joints can move. They help to maintain the stability of the skeleton.

- Tendons — connect muscles to bones. They allow bones to move when muscles contract.

You should take all of this to heart...

In this section, you'll see how the cardiorespiratory system and musculoskeletal system change as you take part in a warm-up. More lasting changes of long-term fitness training are covered in Component 3.

Planning a Warm-Up

Warming up prepares your body systems for exercise — it has tons of benefits.

An Effective Warm-Up has Three Stages

A warm-up gets your body and mind ready for exercise. There are three stages:

pulse raiser ➜ mobiliser ➜ preparation stretches

A Pulse Raiser Gets You Moving

Increased heart rate and oxygen supply are responses from the body systems — see below.

1) A warm-up should start with a pulse raiser, which is activity that gradually increases in intensity to increase the heart rate (number of beats per minute).
2) This eases your body into exercising and increases the oxygen supply to the muscles.
3) Pulse raiser activities include things like jogging, skipping or cycling. It should be specific to the sport and the needs of the participants.

EXAMPLES

Gymnastics — children
Play a game of 'traffic lights'. Children jog when 'green' is said, walk on 'amber' and do a standing balance on 'red'.

Boxing — adolescents
Skip with a rope and do some shadow boxing (practise punching the air against an imaginary opponent).

Wheelchair tennis — adults with physical impairments
Slalom between some cones. Then, rally with a partner on a smaller court.

Our Body Systems Respond to a Pulse Raiser

Cardiorespiratory System

As you increase the exercise intensity in a pulse raiser, there is a response (change) from the cardiorespiratory system:

- heart rate increases — the heart works harder to pump oxygenated blood to the muscles.
- breathing rate increases — you breathe faster to take in more air.
- depth of breathing increases — you breathe more heavily (you take in more air per breath).
- oxygen supply to the working muscles increases — taking in more air means there is more oxygen for the muscles, and the increased blood flow can carry the extra oxygen.
- more carbon dioxide removed from the working muscles — the increased blood flow means more carbon dioxide can be carried to the lungs and breathed out of the body.

Musculoskeletal System

There is also a response from the musculoskeletal system when performing a pulse raiser:

- temperature of muscles increases — as working muscles contract, they generate heat and begin to warm up.
- pliability of muscles increases — warmer muscles are more pliable (elastic), which means they can move more freely.
- reduced risk of muscle strain — more pliable muscles help to reduce the chance of getting a muscle strain (pulled muscle).

Planning a Warm-Up

A Mobiliser Moves Joints through their Full Range of Motion

1) Mobiliser activities come after the pulse raiser.
2) These activities are at a lower intensity and take joints through their full range of movement.
3) Movements should start small and get gradually larger as the warm-up progresses.
4) The joints should be targeted to match the movements of the sport or physical activity.

EXAMPLES

Arm circles could be used by a tennis player to warm up the shoulder joint.

Hip circles can help distance runners to warm up the hips.

Our Body Systems Respond to a Mobiliser

Cardiorespiratory System

1) Since the intensity is lower than the pulse raiser, there is less demand for oxygen by the muscles.
2) This means there is a slight drop in both the heart rate and the breathing rate.

Musculoskeletal System

1) There is increased production of synovial fluid (see p.23) in the joints.
2) This increases lubrication of the joints, which allows the joints to move more smoothly and have a larger range of movement.

Preparation Stretches can be Static or Dynamic

1) The final stage of a warm-up includes preparation stretches.
2) The aim of this stage is to stretch the main muscles that will be used in the sport or physical activity.
3) There are two types of stretch:

Static stretches — stretches performed without moving. You extend a muscle to its furthest point and hold the position (often for 10-15 seconds).

Dynamic stretches — stretches performed with movement, e.g. lunges or high kicks.

4) Stretches should always be done with control and should not cause any pain. Overstretching can cause injury, so you should not push yourself too far.

Planning a Warm-Up

Learn Some Stretches for the Different Muscle Groups

1) A warm-up can include <u>simple stretches</u> or <u>compound stretches</u>.
2) <u>Simple stretches</u> target <u>one muscle</u> at a time, e.g. a standing hamstring stretch.
3) <u>Compound stretches</u> stretch <u>multiple muscle groups</u> at a time,
   e.g. walking lunges stretch the glutes, hip flexors, hamstrings and quadriceps.
4) You need to know <u>stretches</u> for the <u>main muscles</u> (see p.24). Here are some examples:

Bear hug stretch
<u>Dynamic</u> stretch for the <u>deltoids</u>.
Reach your arms out wide, then bring your arms across your chest to hug yourself, squeezing the shoulders.

Overhead arm stretch
<u>Static</u> stretch for the <u>triceps</u>.
Raise your elbow and reach towards the upper back. Pull the elbow back with your free hand and hold.

Cobra stretch
<u>Static</u> stretch for the <u>abdominals</u>.
Lie on your tummy, then push up with your hands to lift your head and chest off the ground.

Standing foot hold
<u>Static</u> stretch for the <u>quadriceps</u>.
Stand with one hand against a wall. Bend one leg and pull your foot towards the buttocks, keeping the knees together.

Calf raises
<u>Dynamic</u> stretch for the <u>gastrocnemius</u>.
Extend the ankle and rise up on to the toes, then lower back down with control.

Sit and reach
<u>Static</u> stretch for the <u>hamstrings</u>.
Sit on the floor with legs out in front of you. Reach out as far as you can and hold still.

Our Body Systems Respond to Preparation Stretches

Cardiorespiratory System

- For <u>static stretches</u>, the <u>heart rate</u> and <u>breathing rate</u> slightly <u>drop</u> as the <u>intensity</u> is even <u>less</u> than it was for the <u>mobiliser activities</u>.
- <u>Dynamic stretches</u> involve more <u>movement</u>, so the <u>heart rate</u> and <u>breathing rate</u> remains at a <u>more elevated level</u>.

Musculoskeletal System

<u>Stretching</u> the muscles increases their <u>range of movement</u> and <u>improves performance</u>. Muscles will be <u>warmer</u> and more <u>pliable</u>, so muscle <u>tears</u> and <u>strains</u> are <u>less likely</u> during the main sport or physical activity.

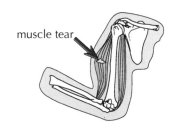

muscle tear

I prefer to warm up with a hot chocolate and an open fire...

It shouldn't come as a surprise that exercise makes you breathe more heavily and your heart pump harder. But you need to know <u>why</u> this happens — it's to increase oxygen supply to the working muscles.

Adapting a Warm-Up

So you've thought of a great warm-up, but you may have to adapt it to meet the needs of your participants.

You can Vary Elements of a Warm-Up

1) A warm-up should be adapted to suit the ages, fitness levels and abilities of participants.
2) This can involve changing the intensity, impact, timing and the types of stretch used.
3) In general, older people, beginners and participants with low fitness levels may need to spend longer warming up and use simpler stretching exercises.

Intensity is a Measure of Difficulty

1) Intensity is how hard someone is working.
2) You can increase intensity by using faster, larger movements or more muscle groups.
3) You can also introduce weights or resistance, e.g. a weighted vest, so participants have to work harder.
4) Low-intensity activities include walking, skipping and jogging.
5) High-intensity activities include running and full-body movements.

Vigorous exercise is hard — you can't talk while doing it.

Moderate exercise is easier — you can talk, but can't sing.

EXAMPLE

For a ballet pulse raiser, you could increase intensity by doing full-body exercises, such as jumping jacks, and leg kicks using ankle weights.

The Surface and Type of Exercise Affects Impact on Joints

1) Impact is a measure of the amount of force exerted on the joints of the body.
2) Running on hard surfaces, such as concrete, is high-impact as it puts a lot of pressure on the knee and ankle joints.
3) Low-impact activities include walking, swimming and cycling.
4) High-impact activities include running, jumping and squats.

EXAMPLE

For a distance running pulse raiser, you could decrease impact by warming up on a softer surface such as grass and reducing the speed of movements to a jog.

Adjust the Length of Time as Needed

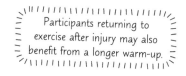
Participants returning to exercise after injury may also benefit from a longer warm-up.

1) The length of time for a warm-up can also be adapted.
2) A typical warm-up may take around 5 to 10 minutes.
3) Older adults and participants with low fitness should spend a longer time on the warm-up (e.g. 10 to 15 minutes) because they have a greater risk of injury.
4) Beginners may also need more time if they are not familiar with the stretches and movements involved in the warm-up.

Adapting a Warm-Up

Simple Stretches are Ideal for Beginners

1) Simple stretches (see p.27) are best to use with beginners. It is easy to focus on the correct technique when only one muscle is being stretched.

2) You can introduce compound stretches with moderate or advanced participants because they can perform basic stretches correctly with less guidance.

EXAMPLES

Beginner sprinters could do a simple standing quadriceps stretch.

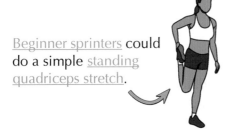

Experienced sprinters could progress to a compound kneeling stretch to work the quadriceps and hip flexors.

Warm-Ups Should be Sport-Specific

A warm-up should always be made relevant to the sport or physical activity. There are three ways that you can make a warm-up more suitable:

(1) Introduce equipment

A pulse raiser should use the same equipment as the sport or physical activity. For example, cyclists should use a bicycle or an indoor exercise bike, and basketball players could jog whilst dribbling a basketball.

(2) Replicate movements

A pulse raiser or mobiliser (see p.26) should use the same movements as those used in the sport or physical activity. For example, gymnasts could perform spins, leaps and turns on the floor, and long jumpers could do exercises that mimic run-up and take-off techniques.

(3) Stretch appropriate muscles

Preparation stretches should target the main muscles that are used in the sport or physical activity. For example, footballers should mostly do stretches for the leg muscles (quadriceps, gastrocnemius and hamstrings), whereas golfers should focus on shoulder muscles (deltoids) and back muscles (erector spinae).

Power napping — for when napping isn't intense enough...

A beginner swimmer should perform a very different warm-up to an elite-level tennis player — you have to know how to adapt warm-ups to make them more suitable for both the sport and a participant's needs.

Delivering a Warm-Up

For Component 1, you'll have to show evidence that you can successfully deliver a warm-up.
You'll need to show good organisation and demonstration skills, and support participants where necessary.

Warm-Ups should be Organised in Advance

1) It's important to plan a warm-up and have everything ready in advance.
2) This means you aren't wasting any time when your participants arrive.
3) You need to consider the factors below, so that the warm-up runs smoothly.

Space

- What facilities will you need to use?
- Is the space indoors or outdoors?
- Can you adapt the warm-up for different weather conditions?
- Is the space large enough for the number of participants? ⬅ You won't always have access to the whole area, e.g. an outside pitch or sports hall.
- Is the space safe (e.g. clear of obstacles)?
- Will you need to mark out any areas with cones or will you use lines on the floor?

Equipment

- What equipment will participants need (e.g. balls, cones, bibs)?
- Is there enough equipment for each participant?
- What equipment will you need to manage participants (e.g. timer, whistle)?

Organisation of participants

- How many participants do you have?
- How experienced are they?
- Will participants work individually or in groups?
- How will you get participants into groups?

Timing

- How long will each stage be (pulse raiser, mobiliser, preparation stretches)?
- How will you know when to move on to the next stage?

EXAMPLE

Football warm-up for a group of 10 adolescents (intermediate level)

Pulse raiser: jogging, shuttle runs (increasing in intensity) and passing in partners.
Mobiliser: hip circles, gate openers (groin), ankle rotations (3 sets of 10 for each).
Preparation stretches: dynamic lunges, side shuffles, static leg stretches.

- Space: 20 m × 20 m area of a 4G pitch, marked out with cones.
- Equipment: 8 × cones, 5 × footballs, 1 × whistle, 1 × stopwatch.
- Organisation of participants: Participants to jog and do shuttle runs as a whole group.
  For the passing activity, split the group into pairs and give each pair a ball.
  Participants to stop and listen to the coach when a whistle is blown.
- Timing: pulse raiser (5 minutes), mobiliser (3 minutes), preparation stretches (3 minutes).

Delivering a Warm-Up

All Participants Must be Able to See the Coach

1) You will need to <u>demonstrate</u> the <u>movements</u> and <u>stretches</u> included in your warm-up.

2) This is particularly important for <u>children</u> or <u>beginners</u>, who may need <u>visual aids</u> to understand what to do.

3) <u>Verbal instructions</u> should also be used when demonstrating.

4) The <u>position</u> of the coach is also very important — you should position yourself so:

- all <u>participants</u> can see <u>you</u> (to correctly <u>copy</u> any <u>demonstrations</u>).
- <u>you</u> can see all <u>participants</u> (to <u>support</u> those that need <u>help</u> — see below).

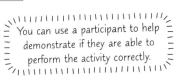

You can use a participant to help demonstrate if they are able to perform the activity correctly.

Give Clear Instructions and Provide Feedback

You should <u>support participants</u> as they perform a warm-up:

Observe participants

1) <u>Position</u> yourself so that you can <u>see all participants</u>.

2) This will allow you to <u>spot</u> any participants who are <u>not</u> using the <u>correct techniques</u> in the warm-up.

Provide instructions

1) Give <u>loud</u>, <u>clear</u> and <u>concise</u> instructions, so participants know what is <u>expected</u> of them.

2) This ensures participants do exercises and stretches <u>correctly</u> and <u>safely</u>, and you don't waste any time <u>repeating yourself</u>.

Provide teaching points

1) A <u>teaching point</u> is <u>technical advice</u> on how to perform an exercise correctly.

2) <u>Effective</u> teaching points are <u>short</u> and <u>specific</u>, so they are <u>easy</u> to <u>remember</u>.

3) For example, teaching points for the <u>downward dog yoga pose</u> may include:
- press into the ground with hands
- keep feet hip width apart
- relax the neck

Provide feedback

Coaches often 'sandwich' feedback by giving praise, constructive feedback, then more praise.

1) <u>Feedback</u> is the <u>response</u> from a coach on how a participant is <u>performing</u>.

2) Give immediate <u>positive feedback</u> (<u>praise</u>) to support <u>good techniques</u> and <u>effort</u>...

3) ...and <u>constructive</u> (or corrective) <u>feedback</u> on <u>specific areas</u> for the participant to improve.

4) Giving <u>both</u> positive and constructive feedback keeps a participant <u>motivated</u>.

Stand and deliver! ...your teaching points and your feedback...

That's Component 1 out of the way. These last two pages are important as you'll revisit the same ideas in Component 2 (leading drills and practices). Make sure you're happy with everything before you continue.

Physical Fitness

Physical fitness is part of being healthy — you can break it down into six different components.

Aerobic Endurance — Supplying the Muscles with Oxygen

Definition: the ability of the cardiorespiratory system to supply oxygen to the muscles, so that the whole body can be exercised for a long time.

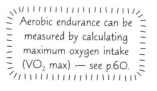
Aerobic endurance can be measured by calculating maximum oxygen intake (VO_2 max) — see p.60.

1) Your heart and lungs work together to provide oxygen and nutrients to the working muscles to delay fatigue.
2) This allows your muscles to work for longer at a low to medium intensity.
3) Most sports require good aerobic endurance. For example, a squash player needs to keep up a fast pace all game. If they get tired too quickly, they could lose points late on in a match.
4) Aerobic endurance is particularly important for endurance sports like long-distance running or cycling.

Muscular Endurance — How Long Until You Get Tired

Definition: the ability to repeatedly use muscles over a long period of time.

1) When your muscles have been overworked, they get tired and start to feel heavy or weak.
2) Muscular endurance allows them to continue to contract (work) at a light to moderate intensity without getting tired.
3) This is important in activities where you're using the same muscles over and over again — e.g. in tennis where you repeatedly swing your arm, and in rowing where repeated strokes propel a rower through the water.

Muscular Strength — the Force a Muscle can Produce

Definition: the maximum force (in kg) that can be generated (made) by a muscle.

1) Muscular strength is just how strong your muscles are.
2) It's very important in sports where you need to lift, push or pull things using forceful movements, e.g. weightlifting, judo or tackling in rugby.
3) Sports that involve holding your own body weight also need a lot of muscular strength — like the parallel bars and rings in gymnastics.

Physical Fitness

Speed — How Quickly

Definition: <u>distance moved</u> per unit of <u>time</u>.

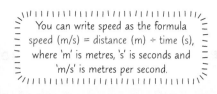

You can write speed as the formula speed (m/s) = distance (m) ÷ time (s), where 'm' is metres, 's' is seconds and 'm/s' is metres per second.

1) <u>Speed</u> is how <u>quickly</u> you can do something.
2) This might be how quickly you <u>cover a distance</u>. It could also be how quickly you can <u>carry out a movement</u>, e.g. how quickly you can throw a punch.
3) To work out speed, you just <u>divide</u> the <u>distance</u> covered by the <u>time</u> taken to do it.
4) Speed is important in lots of activities. E.g. in the <u>100 m sprint</u>, having a <u>greater speed</u> will help you <u>win</u> the race. In <u>hockey</u>, swinging the arm with <u>more speed</u> will whack the ball <u>further</u>.

Flexibility — Range of Motion

He'll bend over backwards to help you, you know.

So I've heard.

Definition: the <u>range</u> of <u>motion</u> possible at a <u>joint</u>.

1) Flexibility means <u>how much movement</u> your joints have. This depends on the <u>type of joint</u> and the '<u>stretchiness</u>' of the <u>muscles</u> around it.
2) Flexibility is often forgotten about, but being flexible has lots of <u>benefits</u>:

- **Improvements in technique** — good flexibility is needed for some activities, e.g. doing the <u>splits</u> in <u>gymnastics</u>. It also means you need to use <u>less energy</u> in other sports, e.g. <u>swimmers</u> with good flexibility can move their arms <u>further</u> around their <u>shoulders</u>. This makes their strokes <u>longer</u> and <u>smoother</u>.
- **Fewer injuries** — it makes you less likely to <u>pull</u> or <u>strain</u> a muscle.
- **Better posture** — more flexibility means a better posture and fewer <u>aches</u> and <u>pains</u>.

Body Composition — Amount of Fat, Muscle and Bone

Definition: the amount of <u>fat mass</u> compared to <u>fat-free mass</u> in the body.

Two people can <u>weigh</u> the same, but have different amounts of body fat.

1) <u>Body composition</u> is just what your body is made of.
2) This includes <u>body fat</u> and <u>fat-free mass</u>, like <u>muscle</u> and <u>bone</u> (and everything else).
3) The <u>ideal</u> amount of body fat depends on your <u>age</u> and <u>sex</u>, e.g. <u>15%</u> to <u>20% body fat</u> is healthy for <u>young women</u>.
4) Having too much body fat can put <u>pressure</u> on your <u>joints</u> during physical activity.
5) Different sports performers have <u>different ideal ratios</u> of fat to fat-free mass:

Sumo wrestlers have <u>lots of fat mass</u> and <u>less fat-free mass</u>, so they are <u>harder</u> to <u>push</u> out of the ring.

Marathon runners have <u>less fat mass</u> and a <u>greater proportion</u> of <u>fat-free mass</u>. Gaining <u>fat mass</u> would <u>slow</u> them down.

I like to think my body composition is 20% fat, 80% hero...

List some different sports and then write down the components of fitness that are useful in each sport. It might not be as fun as taking part in the sports themselves, but it'll come in useful for the assessment.

Skill-Related Fitness

Now it's time to look at <u>five</u> components of fitness that are <u>skill-related</u>. Just like for the physical fitness components, you need to be able to judge their <u>importance</u> for different activities.

Power — Speed and Strength Together

<u>Definition</u>: the <u>product</u> of (result of multiplying) <u>speed</u> and <u>strength</u>.

1) <u>Power</u> is a <u>combination</u> of both <u>speed</u> and <u>strength</u>.
2) High power is needed for <u>explosive movements</u> (quick movements that use a lot of force).
3) Most sports need power. Here are some examples:

Sport	You need power to...
Football	...shoot
Golf	...drive
Tennis	...serve and smash
Cricket	...bowl fast and bat

4) <u>Coordination</u> and <u>balance</u> (see next page) also help make the most of power — an <u>uncoordinated</u> or <u>off-balance</u> action will not be as powerful.

Agility — Being Able to Change Direction Quickly

<u>Definition</u>: the ability to <u>change direction quickly</u> without losing <u>balance</u>.

1) <u>Agility</u> is about changing <u>direction</u> while staying in <u>control</u>.
2) <u>Agile</u> performers can <u>get up</u> off the ground quickly (e.g. after being <u>tackled in rugby</u>) or <u>outmanoeuvre</u> (<u>dodge</u>) other players.
3) Agility is really important for <u>dribbling past opponents</u> in sports like <u>football</u> or <u>hockey</u>.

Reaction Time — The Time It Takes You to Respond

<u>Definition</u>: the <u>time</u> that it takes for a sports performer to <u>react</u> to a <u>stimulus</u> and <u>start</u> their <u>response</u>.

1) A <u>stimulus</u> is a <u>change</u> in the <u>environment</u>.
2) For example, a stimulus can be the noise from a <u>starter gun</u> or a <u>serve</u> in tennis. The <u>time</u> taken for you to <u>start running</u> or start moving to <u>return the serve</u> would be your <u>reaction time</u>.
3) A fast reaction can give you a <u>head start</u> in a race.
4) It is also important in sports where you need to make <u>quick decisions</u> based on what your <u>opponent does</u>, e.g. avoiding a <u>punch</u> in <u>boxing</u> or <u>saving a shot</u> in <u>football</u>.

Skill-Related Fitness

Balance — More Than Not Wobbling

Definition: the ability to keep your centre of mass over a base of support.

1) All objects (including us) have a centre of mass.
2) As you change body position, the location of your centre of mass will change too.
3) You need to have your centre of mass over whatever is supporting you (your base of support) to balance.
4) If you don't have your centre of mass over your base of support, you'll fall over.
5) There are two types of balance:

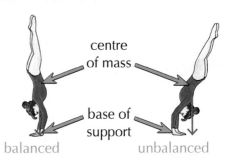

balanced   unbalanced

Static Balance:
This is where the performer is still. For example, when a gymnast is doing a handstand or a headstand.

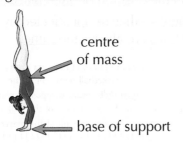

Dynamic Balance:
This is where the performer is moving. For example, when a gymnast is doing a cartwheel.

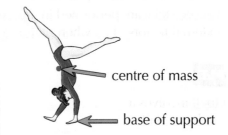

6) Balance is needed for nearly every physical activity. Any sport that involves changing direction quickly, such as canoe slalom, needs good balance.

Coordination — Using Body Parts Together

Definition: the ability to move two or more body parts at the same time, smoothly and efficiently (wasting as little energy as possible).

1) Coordination helps you walk, run, dance, kick, swim...
2) Hand-eye coordination is important for accurate (correct) movements. E.g. being able to hit a ball in tennis or catch a ball in rounders.
3) Coordinated movements are smooth and efficient. E.g. a runner with well-coordinated arms and legs will be able to run faster than someone who is less coordinated.
4) Coordination is really important in sports like gymnastics or platform diving, where your performance is based on your coordination.

My mum says my balance is outstanding... (I owe her money)...

You've now seen all the components of physical fitness and skill-related fitness. Make sure you know what each component is and the types of activities it is important for (and revisit any that you aren't sure about).

Skills and Practice

Skills and practice go hand in hand. You won't be able to develop your skills without practising them.

Each Sport Needs a Different Combination of Skills

1) Skills are learned talents or abilities needed to perform a sport.
2) The level of a performer's skills will affect how well they're able to perform.
3) There are different classifications (types) of skill:

Basic and Complex Skills

- Basic skills are 'simple' skills that are used in many different sports. These include running, throwing, catching or jumping.
- Complex skills are more difficult as they combine basic skills together. These skills are specific to each sport, e.g. bowling in cricket.

Open and Closed Skills

- Open skills are performed in a changing environment — the performer reacts to external factors. E.g. passing in football depends on the position of other players.
- Closed skills are performed in a predictable environment — they're not affected by external factors. E.g. when platform diving, the conditions are always the same.

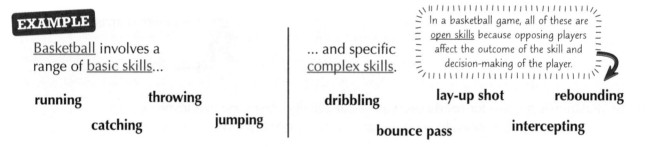

EXAMPLE

Basketball involves a range of basic skills...

... and specific complex skills.

In a basketball game, all of these are open skills because opposing players affect the outcome of the skill and decision-making of the player.

running   throwing   dribbling   lay-up shot   rebounding

catching   jumping   bounce pass   intercepting

Strategies and Tactics Help Develop Performers' Decision-Making Skills

1) Strategies and tactics are plans to improve the chance of a performer or team winning:

   Strategy — a long-term plan for how to achieve an aim, e.g. winning a tournament.

   Tactics — a short-term plan for a specific situation, e.g. how to beat a particular opponent.

2) Strategies and tactics are planned before competition, usually by a coach. They are adapted if they aren't effective.
3) For example, in American football, the offence coach and the defence coach will have tactics for their specific players, which will change each week to match their opponents.
4) Decision-making is done by performers during competition:

   Decision-making — making choices based on external factors, e.g. an ultimate frisbee player deciding when to pass to a teammate.

5) These decisions often need to be made very quickly, e.g. deciding which shot to play in cricket.
6) A performer with good decision-making skills will generally perform better than a performer with poor decision-making skills.

Skills and Practice

Practising Individual Skills Will Improve Your Technique

Isolated practice

Definition: practice where only one skill at a time is worked on.

1) Isolated practice works best when it's for a skill that can be easily repeated, e.g. a sprinter setting off from the starting blocks.

2) The repetition helps you to build muscle memory and will result in you being able to use the skill without thinking about it.

3) Starting a training session with some isolated practice can be a good way to warm up specific muscle groups.

There are advantages and disadvantages of doing isolated practice:

Advantages and Disadvantages:

Advantages:
- There's no pressure, which is good for beginners to gain confidence.
- You can focus on skills that need more practice.
- Some skills can be practised without needing other people.

Disadvantages:
- Doing a skill in a game is very different to doing it in practice.
- It can be boring doing the same thing repeatedly.
- It can take a lot of time to practise each skill individually.

Competitive Situations are a Chance to Test Your Skills

1) Competitive situations are very different to isolated practice — there can be an audience, more pressure and factors that you can't control, such as what your opponents do.

2) Practice games are a good way of replicating the competitive situations of a real game.

3) For example, a real game of hockey would have:

- **Players**: 11 players and 3 substitute players per team.

- **Officials**: Two umpires to enforce the correct rules of hockey.

- **Area of play**: A grass or artificial pitch that is regulation size (see p.42).

4) A practice game may have fewer players (e.g. 5 players per team) and use a smaller area of play (e.g. a half-size pitch) to build confidence.

5) A practice game can be made to feel more like a real competition by using the correct number of players, officials and a proper area of play.

6) You could also invite people to watch, or use performance analysis equipment (see p.21) to increase the amount of pressure that performers feel.

I'm good at dribbling — especially when I fall asleep on the couch...

You'll need to be able to demonstrate a range of skills and strategies for a chosen sport in the assessment, so grab some gear and get practising. Some skills can take a while to improve, so be patient with yourself.

Officials in Sport

The roles and responsibilities of officials depend on the sport being played. However, there's one responsibility that is always the same — making sure that competition is fair and rules are followed.

Most Sports have a Referee or an Umpire

1) Some sports have referees and other sports have umpires — but they have a similar role.

2) They follow the action closely during competition and make decisions based on the rules of the sport, e.g. deciding if a tackle in rugby is legal.

Sports with referees:
- football
- fencing
- boxing
- basketball
- handball
- lacrosse

Sports with umpires:
- hockey
- cricket
- tennis
- netball
- baseball
- bowls

> I'm more of a jump–ire.

3) Referees and umpires are often helped by assistant referees and umpires.

4) They support the main official with decisions, e.g. assistant referees in football make offside decisions, and line umpires in tennis call when a ball is hit out of play.

Other Officials include Judges, Scorers and Timekeepers

Judges

1) Sports like gymnastics, dressage and figure skating are officiated by judges.

2) These sports are subjective — judges score performances based on things such as difficulty and presentation.

3) The number of judges depends on the sport, e.g. there is a panel of 7 judges for major diving events, with the highest and lowest scores ignored.

> Boxing has an in-ring referee to manage the fight and three ring-side judges who score boxers to decide the winner.

Scorers

1) Netball, basketball and cricket have officials called scorers.

2) Scorers keep an accurate record of points scored during a game and update scoreboards.

Timekeepers

1) Netball, boxing and motorsports (e.g. Formula 1) are examples of sports with timekeepers.

2) Timekeepers keep track of time intervals in a sport, e.g. how long a game pauses for, or how quickly a racing driver does a lap.

3) Even though timekeeping is often done electronically, there are still specific officials for it.

Video Review Officials use Technology

> You also covered this in Component 1 — see p.20.

1) Video review officials use technology to make decisions to assist the main officials.

2) There are many different technologies used:

- **Hawk-Eye** — used in sports like tennis to track the trajectory of the ball.
- **Ultra-Edge** — uses small microphones to see if a ball touches the bat in cricket.
- **Video replays** — e.g. used in American football, rugby and basketball to review a passage of play that's just happened (often in slow motion).

Officials in Sport

Officials Have Specific Uniforms

1) Officials wear a <u>specific uniform</u> that is usually set by the <u>National Governing Body</u> of the sport.

2) The uniform is <u>different</u> to what the <u>performers</u> are wearing — this makes them <u>stand out</u>.

3) This is <u>important</u> in team games where many performers are on the <u>field of play</u> at the <u>same time</u>.

EXAMPLES

- Football referees often wear <u>bright yellow shirts</u> and <u>black shorts</u>.
- Ice hockey umpires wear <u>black and white striped shirts</u> with <u>black trousers</u>.
- Boxing referees usually wear <u>white or blue buttoned shirts</u>, <u>black bow ties</u> and <u>black trousers</u>.
- Tennis umpires at <u>Wimbledon</u> wear <u>smart uniforms</u>, including a <u>blazer</u>.

Each Sport has Officiating Equipment

1) Officials also need <u>officiating equipment</u> to help them <u>do their jobs</u>.

2) This equipment helps them to <u>enforce</u> the rules and regulations of the sport.

EXAMPLES

- <u>Referees</u> in rugby use <u>whistles</u> to <u>stop and start play</u>, <u>coloured cards</u> to <u>maintain discipline</u> and a <u>watch</u> to <u>time the game</u>.
- <u>Assistant referees</u> in football use <u>flags</u> when <u>play should stop</u> (e.g. after a foul or an offside call) and an earpiece to <u>communicate</u> with the <u>on-field referee</u>.
- <u>Judges</u> in <u>gymnastics</u> use a <u>pen</u> and <u>paper</u> to note down the <u>skills</u> performed and <u>deductions</u> to take off. They input their scores using a <u>computer</u>.
- <u>Video review officials</u> in <u>cricket</u> need access to <u>Ultra-Edge</u> and <u>Hawk-Eye</u> technology to assist the on-field umpire with decisions.

You've covered officiating equipment in Component 1 — see p.18.

Some Officials Need High Levels of Fitness

1) <u>On-field</u> officials for some sports need high levels of <u>fitness</u> to <u>keep up</u> with <u>performers</u>.

2) They often have to <u>run as much</u> as the performers during a game and must <u>keep close</u> to the action to see <u>exactly</u> what is going on.

3) This allows them to make <u>effective decisions</u>.

4) For example, <u>football referees</u> will need to <u>walk</u>, <u>jog</u> and <u>run</u> for at <u>least 90 minutes</u>, to keep a <u>close eye</u> on the ball at all times.

Officials in Sport

Officials Must be Skilled Communicators

1) Officials must communicate effectively with other officials and performers to make a game run smoothly.

2) Officials must make quick decisions and confidently inform others about their decisions.

3) This includes using clear and concise language.

4) Many sports use hand signals to communicate too, e.g:

- cricket umpires draw a rectangle in the air when they want help from the third umpire.
- football referees point to the penalty spot when awarding a penalty.

Officials Apply Rules and Maintain Control

1) Officials need full knowledge of the rules and regulations of their sport.

2) They must also clearly position themselves to see the field of play and performers at all times, e.g. water polo referees stay next to each play by moving along the side of the pool.

3) This allows them to apply the rules correctly and fairly, and punish any performers that violate the rules.

4) Some decisions can be unpopular, so officials must be assertive and able to explain them if they get questioned.

5) To keep control of performers, officials can:

- verbally warn performers for poor behaviour, e.g. committing a dangerous tackle.
- speak to the team captain and advise them to control the behaviour of their team.
- give official warnings to performers, e.g. a yellow card in badminton, or dismiss a performer from the area of play, e.g. a red card in hockey.

Officials are Responsible for Safety

1) Officials are also responsible for the health and safety of performers.

2) They check equipment and facilities are in a suitable condition before allowing performers on to the field of play.

3) If there is an injury, officials can stop play so the performer can receive medical care.

EXAMPLE

- Football officials check the pitch is safe for players before a match starts (e.g. it is not too wet or icy).
- They also check that players are wearing correct clothing and footwear, e.g. studded boots.

Time out?

What do you call an uncertain referee? An um... pire...

One of the main responsibilities of officials is to stay impartial (not take sides). This is so they can make sure that the decisions they make are fair and don't favour one team or individual over another team or individual.

Rules and Regulations

The rules and regulations of every sport are <u>updated and maintained</u> by its own <u>National Governing Body</u>. The next two pages will look at some rules and regulations of <u>different sports</u>.

Different formats of sports will have different numbers, e.g. 5-a-side football.

Team Sports **have a** Specific Number **of Players**

1) Each <u>team sport</u> has <u>rules</u> on the <u>number of players</u> that can be on the <u>playing area</u> at the <u>same time</u>.
2) Many sports allow <u>substitutions</u> — players who <u>replace</u> another player <u>during</u> a game or match.
3) There may be a <u>fixed number</u> of substitutions or '<u>rolling substitutions</u>', where there is <u>no limit</u> to the number of substitutions that can be made.
4) The table on the right gives some examples.

	No. of players (per team)	Substitutions (per team)
Football	11	5
Water polo	7	6
Curling	4	1
Basketball	5	Rolling

Some Sports Last for a Specific Amount of Time

08:49
12-12

1) Many sports have a <u>set amount</u> of <u>playing time</u>, e.g. <u>90 minutes</u>, with the time split into different periods, e.g. <u>halves</u> or <u>thirds</u>.
2) There can be '<u>overtime</u>' or '<u>extra time</u>' if scores are <u>still level</u> after this period.
3) Other sports have <u>no time limit</u> and <u>play continues</u> until, e.g., a set <u>number of points</u> are reached or a <u>finish line is crossed</u>.

Football also has additional (stoppage) time for injuries etc. which is decided by the referee.

> **EXAMPLE**
>
> 1) In <u>fencing</u>, the <u>maximum length</u> of a contest is <u>9 minutes</u>.
> 2) The contest is <u>split into thirds</u>. Each third lasts <u>3 minutes</u>.
> 3) The <u>contest ends</u> after 9 minutes or once a performer scores <u>15 points</u>.
> 4) There can be <u>1 minute of extra time</u> if the <u>scores are tied</u> after 9 minutes.

There are Different Ways of Scoring in a Sport

Scoring is also assessed by judges (see p.38) in some sports.

1) Sports need a way of <u>deciding</u> who is the <u>winner</u>.
2) This is <u>easy</u> for <u>athletics events</u> — e.g. the winner is the performer who <u>runs 100 m</u> in the <u>fastest time</u>, or <u>throws</u> the furthest in <u>discus</u>.
3) Other sports involve trying to score <u>more goals</u> or <u>points</u> than your opponent.

> **EXAMPLE**
>
> Points can be scored in <u>rugby union</u> in various ways:
>
> - **Try** — <u>5 points</u> for placing the ball <u>behind</u> the <u>opponent's try line</u>.
> - **Conversion** — <u>2 points</u> for <u>kicking</u> the ball <u>through the goalposts</u> after a try.
> - **Drop goal** — <u>3 points</u> for <u>drop-kicking</u> the ball through the goalposts <u>during open play</u>.
> - **Penalty kick** — <u>3 points</u> for kicking the ball <u>through</u> the goalposts <u>after a foul</u>.
> - **Penalty try** — <u>7 points</u> are awarded if the opponent <u>illegally stops a try</u> from being scored.
>
> The team that <u>finishes the game</u> with the <u>most points</u> is the <u>winner</u>. If both teams have the <u>same score</u>, it is a <u>draw</u>.
>
> However, there <u>must</u> be a winner in some games, e.g. in the <u>knockout stage</u> at the World Cup. There will be rules to determine the winner (e.g. <u>extra time</u> and <u>penalty shoot-outs</u>).

Rules and Regulations

Playing Areas have Certain Dimensions

1) Each sport has <u>permitted dimensions</u> (<u>sizes</u>) of their <u>playing area</u>. This may be a <u>specific size</u> or a <u>range</u>.

2) E.g. a rugby field is 94-100 m <u>long</u> (between try lines) and 68-70 m <u>wide</u>.

3) This ensures <u>competition is fair</u> and performers know <u>what to expect</u> when competing <u>away</u> from home.

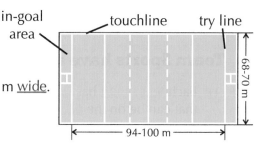

Playing Equipment is Standardised

1) Sports equipment has a <u>standard weight and size</u>, e.g. a cricket ball <u>weighs</u> 156-163 g. However, <u>children</u> often use <u>lighter equipment</u>, e.g. a <u>junior</u> cricket ball <u>weighs</u> 133-144 g.

2) Some sports are <u>dangerous</u> and require <u>protective equipment</u> (see p.17). This makes sure performers are <u>protected</u> from <u>injuries</u>.

3) It is <u>compulsory</u> to wear certain protective equipment in some sports, e.g. <u>gloves</u> in <u>boxing</u>.

4) Other protective equipment is <u>optional</u>, e.g. <u>senior</u> rugby players can <u>choose</u> not to wear mouthguards (but clubs may make it <u>compulsory</u> for <u>junior</u> players to wear them).

There are Rules About How Play can Start and Restart

Each sport has its own rules for <u>starting</u>, <u>stopping</u> and <u>restarting play</u>. Here is an example for <u>squash</u>:

EXAMPLE

- Performers <u>spin a racket</u> or <u>toss a coin</u> to decide who <u>serves first</u>.
- The match is started by the <u>server</u> standing with at least <u>one foot</u> in the <u>service box</u> and then <u>serving</u> the ball.
- After a <u>point is scored</u>, the performer who won the point <u>restarts play by serving</u>.
- <u>Fouls</u> usually happen when one performer accidentally <u>gets in the way</u> of their <u>opponent</u> during a <u>rally</u>. This can result in a <u>let</u> being called (the point is <u>replayed</u>).
- A match typically ends when a player <u>wins three games</u> (each game is <u>first to 11 points</u>).

Performers Get Punished for Not Following the Rules

1) A <u>rule violation</u> is something that <u>goes against the rules</u> of a sport.

2) Some rule violations are <u>sport-specific</u>, e.g. a <u>forward pass</u> in <u>rugby</u> or a <u>double dribble</u> in <u>basketball</u>.

3) Other rule violations are more <u>generic</u>, e.g. hitting a ball <u>out of play</u> or being in an <u>offside position</u>.

4) The consequences for these are <u>minor</u>, e.g. a <u>free kick</u> or <u>possession</u> given back to the <u>other team</u>.

5) Violent behaviour has <u>more serious consequences</u>. Violence towards others results in being <u>sent off the field of play</u> and potentially <u>suspended</u> from the sport for a <u>period of time</u>.

A key role of <u>officials</u> (see p.38-40) is to <u>apply</u> the <u>rules and regulations</u> in a <u>competition</u>. Officials need clear <u>communication</u>, correct <u>use of signals</u> and <u>good positioning</u> to do this effectively.

The drummer who broke the rules had to face the re-percussions...

Rules and regulations are really important to make sports both safe and fair. If all the performers and officials know and follow the rules, then competitions run smoothly with as few interruptions as possible.

Planning Drills and Practices

Drills and practices are important to improve the skills and techniques needed for sport.

Drills are Repetitive Activities to Teach Skills

1) A drill is a repetitive activity used in a training session.
2) The purpose of a drill is to train a specific skill in isolation (by itself).
3) Each sport has its own sport-specific skills that need to be mastered.
4) Some skills are complex, so a whole-part-whole method is often used.
   This is where a whole skill is practised, then broken down into smaller parts.
   E.g. a swimmer can practise front crawl, use a float to focus on
   the kicking action only, then try doing front crawl again.

Drills should Start Simple and get Progressively Harder

Many drills are done progressively — the drill should be easy to start
with, then different elements should be added to increase difficulty.

Unopposed stationary drills

1) Unopposed stationary drills break skills down to their most basic form.
2) These drills are practised while stationary (not moving).
3) Repeating this basic drill will help performers learn the correct techniques.
4) E.g. two performers stand 5 m apart, and throw a rugby ball to each other.

Drills with the introduction of travel

1) You can add progression to a stationary drill with
   travel (movement), e.g. walking or jogging.
2) Adding travel will help performers develop more complex skills (see p.36).
3) E.g. two performers walk, keeping 5 m apart,
   and throw a rugby ball to each other.

Drills with passive opposition

1) Drills with passive opposition use other people as obstacles.
2) Using passive opposition in a drill means performers
   need to focus on what other performers are doing.
3) E.g. two performers jog, keeping 5 m apart, and throw a rugby ball to each other.
   Another person (passive opposition) slowly walks towards them.

> The passive opposition mustn't actively interfere with the drill itself.

Drills with active opposition

1) A drill with active opposition means that an opponent is actively
   trying to stop the other performers from completing the drill.
2) This puts pressure on the performers and encourages them to think quickly and make decisions.
3) E.g. two performers start at a base of a triangle and another person (active
   opposition) starts at the top of the triangle. The performers try to get past
   their opponent by passing (or pretending to pass) the ball at the right time.

Planning Drills and Practices

Conditioned Practices have Rule Changes to Improve Skills

1) A conditioned practice is a practice game where the rules of a sport are changed to focus on specific skills.

2) This is useful for performers to practise skills in a more realistic environment.

This will usually involve games with fewer players (see p.37).

> **EXAMPLE**
>
> 1) In netball, you could set up a conditioned practice to focus on accurate passing.
> 2) You alter the rules of a game so that players need to make 5 successful passes before being allowed to shoot.
> 3) Changing the rules to focus on passing means that performers will need to get into better positions to pass and receive the ball.

3) This type of practice allows the coach to observe progress and give appropriate feedback.

Demonstrating a Technique Shows Performers How it Should be Done

1) Demonstrating a technique to performers is usually better than just explaining it to them.

2) It shows performers exactly what they need to do and how they need to do it.

3) Demonstrations can be done live by a coach or another performer, or a video can be watched.

4) Demonstrations are particularly important if performers are learning a new skill, e.g. how and when to release a hammer during the hammer throw.

5) Here are some important things you should do when demonstrating a technique:

- Do the demonstration slowly
- Repeat the demonstration several times
- Make sure everyone can see
- Break down each part of the technique
- Get the performers to copy your movements
- Answer any questions

Teaching Points Help Coaches to Explain Techniques

1) Demonstrating techniques is important, but coaches should also break each technique down into individual teaching points.

2) Teaching points help participants remember how to do a technique correctly and safely, e.g. how to do a successful parry in fencing or a handstand in gymnastics.

3) When teaching new techniques, coaches need to make sure that they use short sentences and highlight the key points of each technique.

4) For example, teaching points for swimmers doing a tumble turn may include:

- breathe on the last stroke before the wall
- tuck your chin on your chest to start rotating
- push hard against the wall with your feet

Dentists also have to do practice drills...

When planning a drill, start by taking a basic skill, like throwing a ball, and then think about elements you can add to increase the difficulty and improve decision-making (e.g. including passive / active opposition).

Leading Drills and Practices

In your assessment, you'll need to lead drills and conditioned practices to improve a specific sporting skill. This involves the same organisation and supporting skills as delivering a warm-up (look back at p.30-31).

Organisation Skills are Needed to Provide Effective Drills and Practices

Bring specific equipment, e.g. cones for dribbling drills — make sure there is enough for everyone.

The space should be large enough and safe for participants.

Demonstrate drills and techniques, making sure everyone can see.

Adapt practice if needed, e.g. use rowing machines instead of rowing on a river or a lake.

Organisation skills

Position yourself so you can see all participants and spot mistakes.

Decide how to organise participants in each drill, e.g. individuals, pairs or groups.

Split the practice session into parts, e.g. warm-up, drills, conditioned practice, cool-down and review.

Use a stopwatch to time each part of the practice.

Also consider the needs of your participants (see p.8-10), e.g. drills should be fun for children.

Each type of drill (see p.43) needs different amounts of organisation:

- Unopposed stationary drills can be done individually or in groups and work in small spaces.
- Drills with travel need more space and observation to make sure participants move safely.
- Drills with opposition need larger groups and longer demonstrations.

You'll Need to Support Participants in Drills and Practices

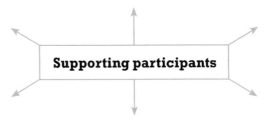

Give clear, concise instructions.

Observe participants to spot strengths and weaknesses.

Explain each drill and answer any questions.

Supporting participants

Give short and simple teaching points for skills and techniques.

Give positive feedback (praise) to keep participants motivated.

Give constructive feedback, so participants know how to improve their technique.

Did you hear about the herb who ran the 100 m? It set a record thyme...

Drills and practices are all about improving the skills of the participants. Having a positive attitude when leading these drills will encourage participants to work hard and will help them to enjoy each session.

Components of Fitness

Look back at pages 32-35 to recap the components of fitness. Over the next three pages, you'll look at some example sports in more detail and the components needed for sports performers to be successful.

It's Important to have High Levels of Fitness

1) Each sport or physical activity needs a different balance of physical and skill-related fitness components.

2) For a particular activity, there will always be some types of fitness which are more important than others — e.g. in weightlifting, your strength is more important than your reaction time.

3) To work out the importance of different types of fitness, think about the kinds of actions the performer does — e.g. a batter in cricket has to respond to the bowler (reaction time), hit the ball (coordination and power), and then run (speed and aerobic endurance).

Physical Components of Fitness Benefit Different Sports...

Component of fitness	Types of sport it benefits	Example
Aerobic endurance	Activities longer than 30 minutes.	Long-distance running
Muscular endurance	Activities longer than 30 minutes.	Long-distance cycling
Muscular strength	Activities needing force.	Hammer throw
Speed	Activities needing fast movements.	100 m hurdles
Flexibility	Activities needing a wide range of movement around a joint.	Judo
Body composition	Different activities need different body compositions.	Gymnastics (low body fat and high muscle mass)

...as do the Skill-Related Components of Fitness

Component of fitness	Types of sport it benefits	Example
Power	Activities needing strong movements.	Gymnastics (vaulting)
Agility	Activities needing quick changes of direction.	Skiing
Reaction time	Activities needing quick decisions or movement in response to a stimulus.	Sprinting
Balance	Activities needing control of your body position to remain steady and upright.	Snowboarding
Coordination	Activities needing the movement of two or more body parts at once.	Tennis

It may also include using sports equipment, such as a tennis racket.

Components of Fitness

You Need to Describe Components of Fitness for Different Activities

Example 1 — Badminton

Agility — players need to change direction quickly, without losing balance when returning shots.

Aerobic endurance — a typical match is longer than 30 minutes, so players need aerobic endurance to keep going for the whole match.

Power — players need power for smash shots that are difficult to return.

Speed — players need to move quickly across the court to return shots.

Coordination — players must hit their shots smoothly and accurately to control where the shuttlecock will land.

Reaction time — players need to react quickly to return fast-paced shots.

Example 2 — Kayaking

Muscular strength — kayakers need strong muscles in their arms and shoulders to produce the force needed to paddle.

Muscular endurance — kayakers need good muscular endurance to constantly use the muscles in their shoulders and arms to paddle.

Power — kayakers need both speed and strength together to paddle quickly and strongly through rough waters.

Balance — kayakers need good balance to stop their kayak from capsizing in rough waters.

Agility — kayakers need to change direction quickly to avoid rocks.

Aerobic endurance — kayakers need good aerobic endurance to paddle for long periods.

Example 3 — Rock Climbing

Power — climbers need power for a 'dyno', which involves pushing off and jumping for a rock that is out of reach.

Muscular strength — climbers need good upper body strength to lift their own body weight.

Flexibility — climbers must stretch for handholds or footholds.

Muscular endurance — climbers must grip rocks and hold their weight for long periods.

Coordination — climbers must carefully position their hands and feet at the same time.

Components of Fitness

Different Events need Different Types of Fitness

Some sports are made up of different events, such as the triathlon. Performers need different types of fitness to perform well in each event.

Gymnasts who compete on all apparatus events need high levels of most of the components of fitness.

Example — Artistic Gymnastics

In men's gymnastics, competitors who perform on the pommel horse need:

Muscular strength — gymnasts need good upper body and core strength to support the body whilst swinging on the handles.

Body composition — gymnasts need to be both light and strong, so have low body fat and high muscle mass.

In women's gymnastics, competitors who perform on the balance beam need:

Balance — gymnasts need good balance to keep their body on the beam and not lose marks for wobbling or falling.

Coordination — gymnasts need coordination to perform controlled moves using different body parts (e.g. spins) to get the best score possible.

Different Positions need Different Types of Fitness

Sometimes, the types of fitness needed can differ between positions in a team sport.

Example — Rugby Union

The backs need:

Agility — backs need to change direction quickly in order to dodge tackles.

Speed — backs need to be able to sprint with the ball to attempt to score a try.

The forwards need:

Muscular strength — forwards need to be strong to take part in the scrum and when tackling to win back possession.

Power — forwards tackle and push with speed and strength.

You've tackled these pages well...

There are lots of sports and each one needs different types of fitness. Study the sports on these pages, then think of your own examples — write down the physical and skill-related components of fitness for each one.

Principles of Training

These pages are all about the principles of training and how they are used in training programmes.

Training Programmes Use Four Basic Principles

1) A training programme is a programme of exercise designed to improve performance.
2) Training programmes are made up of different ways of exercising called training methods.
3) There are four basic principles of training that a coach
   needs to think about when planning a training programme.
4) You can remember these four things using the letters FITT:

> Frequency — How often to train, per week.
>
> Intensity — How hard to train.
>
> Time — How long to train for, each session.
>
> Type — Which training method to use to target the
> component of fitness that needs improving.

Learn the Seven Additional Principles

These seven principles will also help a coach to create a useful training programme.

1. Progressive Overload

Definition: Training that is demanding enough to make the body
adapt (change), leading to improved performance.

1) The only way to get fitter is to work your body harder than normal.
2) This is called overload.
3) You can overload by increasing the frequency, intensity or time you spend training.
4) Your overload needs to be progressive (gradual) — you should only overload a
   little bit at a time, e.g. increase the number of lengths you swim from 25 to 30.
5) If you overload too quickly it can be demotivating or lead to injury.

2. Specificity

Definition: Training should be specific to the individual's sport or activity,
or the physical/skill-related fitness goals to be improved.

1) A coach needs to match training to a performer's sport or fitness goal.
2) For example, if a boxer's fitness goal is to get stronger,
   then they need training methods that build strength.

3. Individual Differences/Needs

Definition: The programme should be designed to meet individual training goals and needs.

For example, an unfit person needs an easier programme than a fitter person, and
a goalkeeper in football would need a different training programme to a striker.

Principles of Training

4. Adaptation

Definition: How the body <u>reacts</u> to <u>training loads</u> by increasing its ability to <u>cope</u> with those loads.

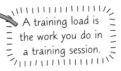

A training load is the work you do in a training session.

1) The <u>work</u> you do in a training session causes your body to <u>change</u> to <u>cope</u> with it.
2) These changes make you <u>fitter</u>.
3) For example, weight training makes your <u>muscles bigger</u>, so you get <u>stronger</u>.
4) Adaptation happens during <u>rest and recovery</u> after a training session.

See p.85-86 for more on how the body adapts to exercise.

5. Reversibility

Definition: If training <u>stops</u>, or the <u>intensity</u> of training is <u>too low</u> to cause <u>adaptation</u>, training effects are <u>reversed</u>.

1) If you <u>stop training</u> (e.g. due to <u>injury</u>), your <u>fitness level</u> will <u>decrease</u> back to how it was before training — it will <u>reverse</u>.
2) Your fitness level will also reverse if you <u>don't train hard enough</u>.
3) In simple terms, if you <u>don't use it</u>, you <u>lose it</u>.

6. Variation

1) It's important to do <u>different activities</u> in training.
2) The sports performer is likely to get <u>bored</u> and <u>lose motivation</u> if they do the <u>same activity</u> over and over again.

7. Rest and Recovery

1) A sports performer needs to <u>rest</u> to allow their body to <u>recover</u> and <u>adapt</u>.
2) During <u>recovery</u> the body <u>repairs</u> any <u>damage</u> caused by exercise.
3) This means the performer will be <u>fit</u> and <u>ready</u> for the next training session.

Just 5 more minutes...

EXAMPLE

A weightlifting coach is designing a training programme.
Describe how they could apply three principles of training in their programme.

Type: the training programme should exercise the <u>muscles</u> that the weightlifter uses, e.g. <u>legs</u>.

Progressive overload: the <u>amount of weight</u> should be <u>gradually increased</u>, so the <u>body adapts slowly</u>.

Rest and recovery: the weightlifter should be <u>given days off</u> between training to <u>recover</u>.

Revisability — keep revising or your braininess will drop...

Want to be fit? Use FITT — Frequency, Intensity, Time and Type. And remember that recovery time is part of training too, because your body needs time to adapt and repair itself, otherwise it can lead to injuries.

Heart Rate and the Borg RPE Scale®

It's useful for sports performers to know how <u>fast</u> their <u>heart</u> is <u>beating</u> during <u>exercise</u>.

Heart Rate shows how Hard you are Working

1) <u>Heart rate</u> (HR) is the number of <u>times</u> the heart <u>beats per minute</u> (bpm).
2) Doing <u>exercise</u> makes the <u>heart beat faster</u> — your heart rate increases to <u>increase</u> the <u>blood</u> (and therefore <u>oxygen</u>) to your <u>muscles</u>.
3) Heart rate can show the <u>intensity</u> a sports performer is <u>working</u> at.
4) The <u>higher</u> their <u>heart rate</u>, the <u>greater</u> the <u>intensity</u> of the exercise.

EXAMPLE

This graph shows an example of a person's heart rate <u>over time</u> during <u>exercise</u>.

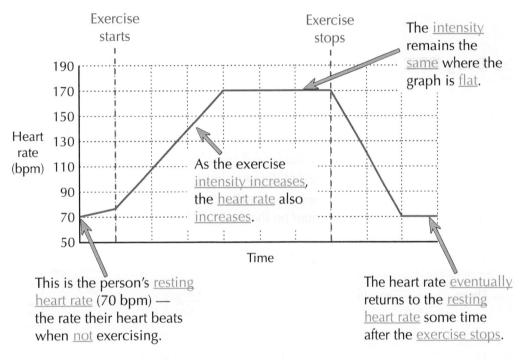

Exercise starts

Exercise stops

The <u>intensity</u> remains the <u>same</u> where the graph is <u>flat</u>.

As the exercise <u>intensity increases</u>, the <u>heart rate</u> also <u>increases</u>.

This is the person's <u>resting heart rate</u> (70 bpm) — the rate their heart beats when <u>not</u> exercising.

The heart rate <u>eventually</u> returns to the <u>resting heart rate</u> some time after the <u>exercise stops</u>.

You Measure Heart Rate Manually or with Technology

1) You can <u>measure</u> your heart rate like this:

   (1) Place your first and second <u>fingers</u> on the <u>artery</u> on the <u>underside</u> of your wrist.

   (2) Using a <u>stopwatch</u>, count the number of <u>pulses</u> in <u>sixty seconds</u>.

   Never use your thumb to take your pulse — it has a pulse of its own.

2) You can also <u>measure</u> your heart rate with a <u>heart rate monitor</u> or <u>smartwatch</u>.
3) <u>Apps</u> are another option — these measure your heart rate using a <u>smartphone's camera</u> and <u>light sensors</u>.

Heart Rate and the Borg RPE Scale®

You can Work Out a Person's Maximum Heart Rate

1) Maximum heart rate (MHR) is the highest number of times that the heart can beat in one minute.

2) Maximum heart rate is also called HR max.

3) You can estimate a person's maximum heart rate using this equation:

$$HR\ max\ (bpm) = 220 - age \Longleftarrow This\ is\ age\ in\ years.$$

> **EXAMPLE**
>
> Estimate the maximum heart rate of a 25-year-old.
>
> HR max = 220 – age (years)
>
> = 220 – 25
>
> = **195 bpm**

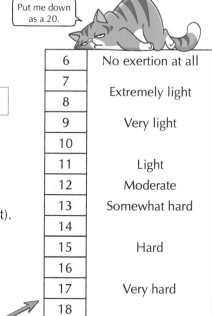

Put me down as a 20.

6	No exertion at all
7	Extremely light
8	
9	Very light
10	
11	Light
12	Moderate
13	Somewhat hard
14	
15	Hard
16	
17	Very hard
18	
19	Extremely hard
20	Maximal Exertion

The Borg RPE Scale® Measures Exercise Intensity

1) Borg was a scientist who studied sport.

2) In 1970, he came up with the Borg (6-20) RPE Scale®.

3) RPE stands for Rating of Perceived Exertion, which is used as a measure of exercise intensity.

4) The numbers on the scale represent different levels of exertion (effort).

5) While a person is exercising they are asked to rate how they feel, by giving a number on the scale.

6) For example, if they feel like the exercise they're doing is very light (easy) they would rate it a 9.

These numbers are the RPE — the ratings of perceived exertion.

The Borg RPE Scale® can Estimate Heart Rate

1) To get a rough idea of heart rate (HR) during exercise, you can use the Borg RPE Scale.

2) To do this, you need to put the rating (RPE) from the Borg RPE Scale into an equation.

3) Here is the equation:

$$HR\ (bpm) = RPE \times 10$$

You can also work out RPE if you know the heart rate. Just do:
$$RPE = HR\ (bpm) \div 10.$$

> **EXAMPLE**
>
> Zara has a Borg Scale rating (RPE) of 17. Estimate her heart rate.
>
> HR (bpm) = RPE × 10
>
> = 17 × 10
>
> = **170 bpm**

It takes maximal exertion just to get myself out of bed...

Heart rate is a great measure of exercise intensity, and it's easy to measure (with or without equipment). People often overestimate how hard they are working, so RPE is a less accurate measure of heart rate.

Heart Rate Target Zones

Keeping your heart ticking within a target zone when training is helpful for improving your fitness.

Aerobic and Anaerobic Activity Depends on the Intensity

Your muscles can release energy in two ways — it depends on how hard you are exercising (intensity).

Aerobic Activity

1) Aerobic activity is 'with oxygen'.
2) When exercise isn't too intense and is at a steady rate, e.g. jogging, your heart and lungs can supply enough oxygen to the working muscles.
3) Muscles release energy using oxygen, and make carbon dioxide as a waste product.

Anaerobic Activity

1) Anaerobic activity is 'without oxygen'.
2) During intense exercise, e.g. sprinting, your heart and lungs can't supply the working muscles with enough oxygen.
3) Muscles release energy without oxygen, and make lactic acid as a waste product.

You can work out the type of activity you are doing by measuring your heart rate — see below.

Heart Rates Should be in a Target Zone when Training

1) A sports performer needs to exercise at the right intensity when training to maximise their improvement in fitness.
2) They can do this by making sure their heart rate is in a target zone.
3) There are different target zones for aerobic and anaerobic training:

AEROBIC TARGET ZONE —
60%-80% of maximum heart rate.

ANAEROBIC TARGET ZONE —
80%-90% of maximum heart rate.

4) The boundaries of the training zones are called training thresholds:

- If you're a beginner, you should train nearer the lower threshold, — so around 60% for aerobic training and 80% for anaerobic training.

- Serious athletes train close to the upper threshold — so around 80% for aerobic training and 90% for anaerobic training.

Some people use 60-85% of HR Max for aerobic training, and 85-95% of HR Max for anaerobic training.

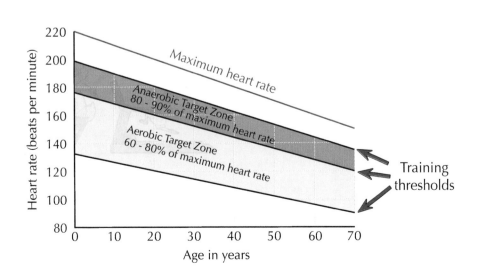

Heart Rate Target Zones

Performers Should Calculate their Target Zone

1) Performers need to work out the ideal target zone to get the most out of a fitness training method.

2) They need to know their maximum heart rate and whether they are doing aerobic or anaerobic training.

3) Look at the example below for how to calculate a target zone for a 20-year-old long-distance cyclist.

EXAMPLE

1 Find the maximum heart rate
Use the equation HR max = 220 – age (see p.52).
220 – 20 = 200, so their HR max is 200 bpm.

2 Find the thresholds
Long-distance cycling is mainly an aerobic activity,
so use the aerobic target zone thresholds.

Aerobic	Anaerobic
Lower = 60% of HR max	Lower = 80% of HR max
Upper = 80% of HR max	Upper = 90% of HR max

For the anaerobic thresholds, you'd use 0.8 and 0.9.

3 Multiply the thresholds by the maximum heart rate
Now calculate the aerobic target zone:
The lower threshold is 60% of the maximum heart rate — that's 200 × 0.6 = 120.
The upper threshold is 80% of the maximum heart rate — so 200 × 0.8 = 160.

So the cyclist's target zone for aerobic training is between 120 and 160 beats per minute.

Your Training Intensity Should Suit Your Activity

1) If you want to be good at an aerobic activity, like long-distance running, then you should do a lot of aerobic endurance training (see p.75) as part of your training.

2) Anaerobic training helps your muscles tolerate (put up with) lactic acid. For anaerobic activity like sprinting, you need to do anaerobic training, e.g. speed training (see p.80).

3) In many team sports, like lacrosse, you need to be able to move about continuously (aerobic) for the whole match, and also have spurts of fast movement (anaerobic).

4) You should have a mix of aerobic and anaerobic activities in your training for these.

I did a workout at a campsite — that was training in tent city...

Make sure you remember the range of percentage values that go with aerobic and anaerobic target zones.
In the exam, you may have to evaluate whether a performer is exercising at the correct intensity.

Repetition Max Tests

Repetition Max (RM) tests are a way of finding your body's upper limits, so you can set goals. It's important to do these tests safely — make sure you have someone with you to act as a spotter when lifting heavy weights.

One Rep Max is the Maximum you can Lift Once

1) A rep (repetition) is one specific movement or exercise. For example, one biceps curl.
2) A good way to find your maximal strength is to do a one rep max (1RM) test.
3) To find your one rep max, you need to find the heaviest weight you can lift safely using a particular muscle group. The heavier this weight, the stronger the muscle group.
4) Start with a weight you know you can lift. Once you successfully lift it, rest for a few minutes.
5) Increase the weight you attempt in small steps until you reach a weight with which you can't complete a single lift. The last weight you managed to successfully lift is your one rep max.

You can also Work Out a Fifteen Rep Max

1) Fifteen rep max (15RM) is the maximum weight you can lift for fifteen reps.
2) To find your 15RM, you need to find a weight that is not too heavy (e.g. start around 50% of your 1RM), then see if you can do fifteen reps.
3) If you cannot do fifteen reps, rest and try again with a lighter weight.
4) If you can do fifteen reps with the weight, rest for a while and increase the weight, then try again. Repeat until you cannot complete the full fifteen.
5) Your 15RM is the heaviest weight you managed to successfully lift fifteen times.

> Resting is very important for RM tests — you won't be able to perform well if your muscles are tired from the last go.

Training Intensity is Defined Using 1RM

You can describe the intensity of strength training (see p.78) as a percentage of the 1RM. For example, if your 1RM is 80 kg, then 50% of your 1RM would be 80 × 0.5 = 40 kg.

Training for Maximum Strength

1) Maximum strength training helps muscles to lift a large amount in one movement.
2) For this training, you need high loads and low reps.

> For example: 3 sets of 6 reps at 90% 1RM.

Training for Muscular Endurance

1) Muscular endurance training helps muscles to keep repeating the same movement.
2) For this training, you need low loads and high reps.

> For example: 5 sets of 20 reps at 50-60% 1RM.

> Or you could give this as a percentage of 15RM.

My last rest between sets lasted 5 years...

1RM tests are not suitable for beginners — lifting with poor form can be very dangerous. Instead, there are many online calculators that estimate 1RM based on the number of reps performed with smaller weights.

Fitness Tests

A coach uses <u>fitness tests</u> to find out about a sports performer's <u>fitness</u>.

Fitness Testing **Helps Identify** Strengths **and Weaknesses**

1) Fitness tests are designed to <u>measure</u> particular <u>components of fitness</u> (see p.32-35).

2) Fitness tests produce <u>data</u> (results), which can be used to:

- Find out the sports performer's <u>baseline</u> (starting) <u>fitness level</u>.
- <u>Design</u> a <u>training programme</u> based on what <u>components of fitness</u> need improving.
- Find out if the <u>training programme</u> is <u>working</u>.
  The sports performer is tested often to see if they are <u>improving</u>.
- <u>Motivate</u> the sports performer and have something to <u>aim</u> for.
- Agree appropriate <u>fitness goals</u> for the sports performer to achieve.

Coaches Need to **Choose** the Right Test

To choose the <u>right fitness test</u>, a coach needs to think about <u>three</u> things:

1. The Test Purpose

1) A coach needs to think about the <u>component of fitness</u> they want to measure. For example, a coach might want to measure an athlete's speed.

2) They need to choose a <u>test</u> that <u>measures</u> this type of fitness.
   For example, the 30 m sprint test (see p.64) is a test that measures speed.

2. The Test Situation

1) A coach needs to think about the <u>practicality</u> of carrying out the test (how possible it is to carry out).

2) Practicality considerations include things like:

- <u>cost</u> — how much does the test cost because of the equipment needed?
  E.g. the timed plank test (p.62) is cheap — it only requires a stopwatch and a mat.
- <u>time taken</u> — how long does it take to set up and perform the test or analyse the data?
  E.g. it takes time to measure out an accurate course for the Illinois agility run test (p.67).
- <u>number</u> of <u>people</u> — how many people can do the test at once?
  E.g. lots of sports performers could all do an MSFT (p.60) at the same time.

3) The <u>most practical</u> tests use <u>cheap / minimal equipment</u> and are <u>set up</u> and <u>carried out quickly</u>.

3. The Needs of the Sports Performer

1) The coach needs to think carefully about the <u>safety</u> of the sports performer.

2) For example, they need to think about the performer's <u>age</u> and <u>health</u>.

3) The sports performer shouldn't do a test where they could get <u>injured</u>.

4) For example, someone who has a <u>bad back</u> shouldn't do a fitness test that uses their <u>back</u>.

You might find this section incredibly testing...

This section is about understanding <u>why</u> fitness tests are important — they help the coach and sports performer monitor progress and set goals. You'll be told <u>how</u> to set up fitness tests later in this Component.

Pre-Test Procedures

Pre-test procedures are things that need to be done before a fitness test.
There are four procedures that you should know.

Equipment Needs to be Calibrated

1) Calibrating equipment means adjusting it to make sure it's set up right and is working properly.
2) For example, scales must be set to zero before a person is weighed.
   If they're not, they need adjusting.
3) Calibration makes sure the readings that are taken are
   accurate (as close to the real value as possible).

Participants Need to Give Informed Consent

1) Participants must be told the purpose of a fitness test
   and what it involves before they agree to take part.
2) Once they know these things, they can agree to take part by signing and
   dating a form before doing the test. This is called informed consent.
3) The participant can also stop doing the test at any time.

Participants Fill in a Questionnaire (PAR-Q)

1) The coach should know if a participant is in good health before doing any fitness tests.
2) This information is usually gathered with a
   Physical Activity Readiness Questionnaire (PAR-Q).
3) It includes questions on a participant's overall health and fitness, for example:

   - Have you ever been told you have a heart condition?
   - Do you feel any chest pain when you do physical activity?
   - Are you on any medication that may affect
     your ability to do physical activity?

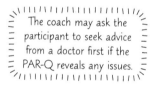
The coach may ask the participant to seek advice from a doctor first if the PAR-Q reveals any issues.

4) A PAR-Q can reveal injuries or illnesses that may prevent a participant from taking
   part in a test safely, and allows the coach to select an appropriate test.

Participants Should do a Pre-Fitness Check

1) Pre-fitness checks also inform a coach about
   a participant's overall fitness and experience.
2) This might involve collecting measurements
   such as height, weight and resting heart rate.
3) There may also be more questions, e.g. to find out the types
   and amount of exercise the participant has done in the past.

Check the box to confirm you're happy to continue ☐ ...

It's really important that coaches have knowledge about a participant's health (with consent of course).
This informs the coach on whether a participant is fit enough to safely carry out the fitness tests.

Carrying Out Fitness Tests

Once a coach has chosen an appropriate test and completed all pre-test procedures, they can carry out the test.

Fitness Tests Should Follow a Standard Procedure

Before you start a fitness test, the participant must warm-up.
Then the standard procedure of the test must be followed:

1) A standard procedure is a set of instructions describing how to do a fitness test.
2) The standard procedure includes the equipment needed for the test.
3) The same standard procedure is used every time, by everyone doing the test.
4) This means that the results can be compared with other people's results and published national norms for age and sex.
5) The standard procedures for each fitness test that you need to know about are on pages 60-71.

Results Must be Recorded Accurately

1) It's important to be accurate when measuring and recording the results of fitness tests.
2) You can do this by:

(1) Choosing the right equipment.
For example, to time something, use a stopwatch instead of the second hand on a watch. This is because a stopwatch is more accurate.

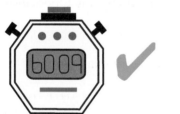 

(2) Always putting results into a data table. This keeps data organised (tidy).

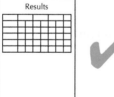 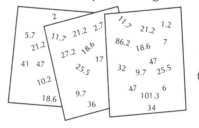

3) It's also important to measure and record your results in the right units, e.g. cm or seconds.
4) This allows your results to be compared to other people's results and published data.

Fitness Tests Give you Data About Your Fitness Levels

1) You can compare your data from fitness tests over time to see how your training is going — e.g. if each week you're recording a bigger distance on a vertical jump test (see p.70), you know you're increasing your leg power.
2) You can also compare your own performance in a fitness test with average ratings. This can tell you how you rate compared to other people for your age and sex.
3) Most fitness tests will have a 'normative' table that you can compare your results with. You can find out more about interpreting your results on page 72.

Carrying Out Fitness Tests

Fitness Tests Need to be Reliable

1) A fitness test is <u>reliable</u> if a sports performer gets <u>consistent results</u> when they <u>repeat</u> the test under the <u>same conditions</u>.
2) <u>Different conditions</u> could make the test results <u>less reliable</u>.
3) These <u>factors</u> affect the reliability of results:

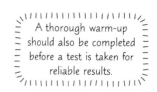
A thorough warm-up should also be completed before a test is taken for reliable results.

- <u>equipment calibration</u> — <u>equipment</u> must be <u>calibrated</u> before each test.

- <u>motivation of participant</u> — a participant must put in the <u>same amount of effort</u> each time.

- <u>environmental conditions</u> — the test should be done on the <u>same surface</u> and in the same <u>weather conditions</u> (if outside).

- <u>experience of coach</u> — the person running the test should <u>know</u> how to carry it out <u>properly</u>.

- <u>compliance with standard test procedure</u> — the <u>standard procedures</u> for the test should be used.

EXAMPLES

<u>Environmental conditions</u>
A sprinter does a <u>speed</u> fitness test <u>twice</u>:
- On the <u>first time</u> the weather is <u>sunny</u> — the <u>ground</u> is <u>dry</u>.
- On the <u>second time</u> it is <u>raining</u> — rain makes the <u>ground slippery</u>.
This makes the test results <u>different</u> and the test <u>unreliable</u>.

<u>Motivation of participant</u>
A climber does a <u>muscular endurance</u> test <u>twice</u>:
- On the <u>first time</u> the climber is <u>tired</u> and has <u>low motivation</u>.
- On the <u>second time</u> the climber is <u>well-rested</u> and <u>wants to do better</u>.
Again, this makes the test results <u>different</u> and the test <u>unreliable</u>.

The Fitness Test has to be Valid

1) A fitness test is <u>valid</u> if it <u>measures</u> the <u>component of fitness</u> that it's <u>supposed to measure</u>.
2) For example, a coach wants to measure the <u>strength</u> of a sports performer's <u>leg muscles</u>. He uses a test that measures the <u>strength</u> of the <u>arm muscles</u> (e.g. grip dynamometer test — see p.65). This test (and the results) are <u>not valid</u> for what the coach wants to measure.

Watch out — if a fitness test isn't <u>set up</u> and <u>done correctly</u>, then it's <u>not reliable</u>. This is <u>different</u> to the test being <u>not valid</u>.

Ah yes, the old "The machine wasn't calibrated properly" excuse...

Just because a test is reliable, it doesn't mean that it's valid — that's true the other way round too. Fitness tests have to be valid and reliable to make sure the data is accurate and useful for a coach.

Aerobic Endurance Tests

The next two pages look at some fitness tests for aerobic endurance. These are suitable for measuring the fitness of long-distance athletes or players of team sports which have lots of running, e.g. football.

The Multi-Stage Fitness Test (MSFT) Involves Shuttles

A Multi-Stage Fitness Test (MSFT) is used to predict a performer's VO_2 max, which is the maximum amount of oxygen the body can use during one minute of exercise.

MSFT — Standard procedure

Equipment: tape measure, cones, MSFT recording and speakers.

1) Two lines, 20 m apart, are marked out using a tape measure.
2) A recording of timed bleeps is played.
3) On the first bleep, the sports performer must run from one line to the next. This is one shuttle. Their foot must be on or over the line when the next bleep sounds.
4) They carry on running shuttles to the sound of the bleeps.
5) The bleep test has different levels. As the level increases, the time between bleeps gets shorter. This means the sports performer must run faster.
6) The test is over if they can't carry on or if they miss three bleeps in a row.
7) The level and number of shuttles completed is the final score.
8) The results are used to find VO_2 max (in ml/kg/min) in a published data table.

Reliability

The lines should be exactly 20 m apart — any slight difference will make the results less reliable.

Validity

If the sports performer stops before they are too tired to carry on, the results aren't valid.

The Yo-Yo Test is Similar to the MSFT

The Yo-Yo Intermittent Recovery Test is often just called the Yo-Yo Test.

Yo-Yo Test — Standard procedure

Equipment: tape measure, cones, Yo-Yo test recording and speakers.

1) Three lines are marked out using a tape measure. The distances between the lines are 5 m and 20 m, as shown on the right.
2) Performers line up on the start line.
3) Timed bleeps are played and performers complete 20 m shuttles, with bleeps getting shorter over time (just like in the MSFT).
4) However, after every two shuttles, there is a 10 second recovery period.
5) During the recovery period, performers must jog to the line 5 m away and back to the start line.
6) Performers are eliminated like in the MSFT, and the score is the level and number of shuttles.
7) The results are used to find VO_2 max (in ml/kg/min) in a published data table.

| ← 5 m → | ←   20 m   → |
| Recovery | Run |

Turn line | Start / Finish line | Turn line

The reliability and validity factors are the same as for the MSFT.

Aerobic Endurance Tests

The Harvard Step Test Uses Step-Ups

For the Harvard Step Test, performers step on and off a step or bench.
Unlike the MSFT and Yo-Yo test, performers don't have to
exercise until they are exhausted and have to stop.

Harvard Step Test — Standard procedure

Equipment: ruler, step, stopwatch, metronome (a device that 'clicks' at regular beats)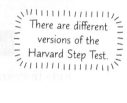

1) Set up a 51 cm step for men or a 41 cm step for women.
2) Performers do 30 step-ups on the step every minute (a step every two seconds) for 5 minutes. (The metronome can help you step at the right pace.)
3) You then take three pulse readings: the first is taken one minute after you finish the test, the second is taken two minutes after and the third is taken three minutes after.
4) You put these numbers into a formula to work out your score. The results are used to find VO_2 max in a published data table.

There are different versions of the Harvard Step Test.

Reliability

1) The correct step height should be used, depending on the sex of the performer.
2) If a performer can't step in time with the metronome, the results will be less reliable.

Validity

People with longer legs may find this test easier, which makes it less valid.

You can Run or Swim the 12-Minute Cooper Test

For the 12-Minute Cooper Test, you'll need a running track or a swimming pool.
This is another aerobic test where performers don't exercise until exhaustion.

12-Minute Cooper Test — Standard procedure

Equipment: stopwatch.

1) Run round the track as many times as you can or swim as far as you can in 12 minutes.
2) The distance you run or swim is recorded in metres. The further you can run or swim, the better your aerobic endurance.
3) The results are used to find VO_2 max in a published data table — the tables for running and swimming are different.

The 12-minute Cooper swim test is (obviously) most suitable for long-distance swimmers.

Reliability

How far a performer runs or swims can vary depending on how motivated they are.

Validity

The test requires the performer to pace themselves, which may mean less experienced performers tire out too quickly.

The Harvard staircase test — a step too far...

If you are able, try out some of the fitness tests yourself so you can experience what performers have to do.
Or you could play the role of a coach and watch someone else do them while you put your feet up...

Muscular Endurance Tests

These fitness tests <u>measure</u> a performer's <u>muscular endurance</u> — they only need a <u>stopwatch</u> and a <u>mat</u>.

One-Minute Tests Measure Endurance of Muscle Groups

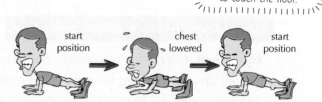

A modified version of the test allows the knees to touch the floor.

One-Minute Press-Up Test — Standard procedure

1) The sports performer <u>begins</u> in the <u>start position</u>.
2) On the word '<u>GO</u>', they <u>lower</u> their <u>chest</u> to the floor keeping their back straight.
3) They then <u>return</u> to the <u>start position</u>. This is <u>one rep</u> (one press-up).
4) Another person counts <u>how many reps</u> the performer does in <u>one minute</u> using a <u>stopwatch</u>.
5) The results of this test are usually given in <u>reps per minute</u> and compared to a <u>published data table</u>.

One-Minute Sit-Up Test — Standard procedure

1) The sports performer <u>lies on the mat</u> in the <u>start position</u>.
2) On the word '<u>GO</u>', they <u>sit up</u>, until their <u>elbows touch their knees</u>.
3) They then lower themselves back down to the <u>start position</u>. This is <u>one rep</u> (one sit-up).
4) Another person counts <u>how many reps</u> the performer does in <u>one minute</u> using a <u>stopwatch</u>.
5) The results of this test are usually given in <u>reps per minute</u> and compared to a <u>published data table</u>.

Reliability

Allowing press-ups or sit-ups with the <u>wrong technique</u> will affect the <u>score</u> (number of reps) on the test.

Validity

1) Each test <u>only</u> measures the <u>muscular endurance</u> of <u>certain areas</u> of the body (<u>upper body/abdominals</u>).
2) It <u>isn't valid</u> as a measure of <u>overall</u> muscular endurance.

The Timed Plank Test Measures Core Endurance

Timed Plank Test — Standard procedure

1) The performer <u>supports</u> the <u>upper body</u> using the <u>elbows</u> and <u>forearms</u>.
2) They <u>straighten their legs</u> and put their <u>weight</u> on the tip of their <u>toes</u>, with their <u>hips lifted</u> off the floor and <u>back straight</u>.
3) Once in position, start the <u>stopwatch</u>. The score is <u>how long</u> it takes <u>before</u> the <u>hips</u> are <u>lowered</u>.
4) The results are compared to values in a <u>published data table</u>.

Reliability

It can be difficult to <u>judge</u> when the performer '<u>fails</u>'.

Validity

The test measures <u>core</u> (<u>central body</u>) muscular endurance, but is not valid for <u>other muscle groups</u>, e.g. leg muscles.

I prefer the log test — it involves lots of sleeping...

Core muscular endurance is a benefit for many physical activities and the timed plank test is a very practical test to measure it — you need minimal equipment and lots of people can take part at once.

Flexibility Tests

The tests on this page measure a sports performer's flexibility.

The Sit and Reach Test Measures Leg and Back Flexibility

Sit and Reach Test — Standard procedure

Equipment: tape measure, box.

1) The sports performer sits on the floor with their legs straight out.
2) A box is placed flat against the sports performer's bare feet.
3) The sports performer reaches forward as far as they can.
4) Another person measures the distance from their feet to where they reach with a tape measure.
5) The sports performer gets three turns. Their best score is recorded.
6) The results of this test are usually given in centimetres (cm) or inches.
7) The results are compared to values in a published data table.

Reliability

1) If the legs are not kept straight during the test, the score will be unreliable.
2) If the sports performer hasn't warmed up before the test, they'll get a worse score than they should.

Validity

1) The test only measures the flexibility of the back and hamstrings. It isn't valid as a measure of overall flexibility.
2) It doesn't account for variations in the length of a performer's arms or legs.

Calf and Shoulder Flexibility Tests are Also Used

Calf Flexibility Test — Standard procedure

Equipment: tape measure, wall.

1) The sports performer stands facing a wall, with one foot in front of the other.
2) They bend the front knee so it touches the wall, keeping both heels on the floor.
3) Measure the distance from the front of the big toe to the wall.
4) The performer moves back and repeats until they fail. The greatest distance without failing is their score.
5) They repeat the test on the opposite leg.

This test has no data table, so you can only compare results against yourself.

Shoulder Flexibility Test — Standard procedure

Equipment: tape measure, skipping rope.

1) The sports performer holds a skipping rope in front of them, with hands shoulder-width apart.
2) They extend the arms over the head and behind them to touch their back. The performer can slide the hands apart just enough to make this possible.
3) Another person measures the shoulder width and distance between the thumbs (in cm), then subtracts the first measurement from the second.
4) The performer gets three turns. Their best score is recorded.
5) The results are compared to values in a published data table.

Reliability

A warm-up of the calves / shoulders is needed for a reliable score in each test.

Validity

1) Each test only measures the flexibility of certain areas of the body (calves / shoulders).
2) It isn't valid as a measure of overall flexibility.

I'm pretty flexible — I'm free Mondays, Tuesdays and weekends...

Good flexibility is useful for most sports. Just remember that these tests are good indicators of flexibility for particular areas, e.g. the hamstrings or shoulders, but don't provide a full picture of a performer's flexibility.

Speed Tests

Here's another page on fitness tests — this time there are two speed tests to learn...

The 30 Metre Sprint Test has a Standing Start

30 Metre Sprint Test — Standard procedure

Equipment: tape measure, cones, stopwatch.
1) 30 metres is marked out on a flat running surface using a tape measure.
2) On the word 'GO', the sports performer runs the 30 metres as fast as they can.
3) Another person uses a stopwatch to time how long it takes.
4) The sports performer gets three turns (with a few minutes to recover in between).
5) Their best score is recorded.
6) The results of this test are usually given in seconds.
7) The results are compared to values in a published data table.

Reliability

1) If the reaction times of the person with the stopwatch are slow, the results will be inaccurate.
2) This makes the results less reliable.

Validity

1) It's a valid test for sports that involve running.
2) It is a less valid test of speed for sports that don't involve running. For example, swimming.

The 30 Metre Flying Sprint Test has a Running Start

The 30 metre flying sprint test is similar to the 30 metre sprint, but performers run another 30 m from a running start.

30 Metre Flying Sprint Test — Standard procedure

Equipment: tape measure, cones, stopwatch.
1) 60 metres is marked out on a flat running surface. Halfway along, another line is marked out to split the surface into two sections of 30 m.
2) On the word 'GO', the sports performer begins running as fast as they can.
3) Another person starts the stopwatch as they pass the 30 m mark and stops the stopwatch at the 60 m mark.
4) This means the performer is timed running the final 30 m from a running start.
5) The sports performer gets three turns (with a few minutes to recover between each one).
6) Their best score is recorded.
7) The results of this test are usually given in seconds.
8) The results are compared to values in a published data table.

The person using the stopwatch can't stand at both the 30 m and 60 m mark, so it is hard to judge when the performer has crossed each line, and results can be unreliable.

Otherwise, the reliability and validity factors are the same as for the 30 metre sprint test.

The athletics club's always having a laugh — must be a running joke...

These two tests start out the same — the performer runs 30 metres from a standing start. But in the flying sprint test, the performer runs for a further 30 m to measure their speed from a running start.

Component 3 — B2: Test Methods for Physical Fitness

Muscular Strength Tests

Get a grip on this page about two muscular strength tests.

A Grip Dynamometer Tests your Grip Strength

Grip Dynamometer Test — Standard procedure

Equipment: grip dynamometer.

1) The sports performer holds the grip dynamometer in their dominant hand. (For example, if they are right handed their dominant hand will be their right hand.)
2) The grip dynamometer is adjusted to fit the size of their hand.
3) The sports performer squeezes as hard as they can for five seconds. The reading is recorded.
4) The sports performer gets three turns (with one minute to recover between each one).
5) Their best score is recorded.
6) The results of the test are given in kilograms (kg) and compared to values in a published data table.

Reliability

If the grip dynamometer isn't adjusted to fit the sports performer's hand size, the results will be less reliable.

Validity

1) The test only measures the muscular strength of the lower arm and hand muscles.
2) This means it is not a valid test for testing the strength of other body parts.

The One Rep Max Test gives your Maximum Muscle Strength

One Rep Max Test — Standard procedure

See p.55 for a reminder on RM tests.

Equipment: free weights or adjustable weight machine.

1) The sports performer attempts one rep of a heavy weight that they know they can lift safely.
2) If they succeed, they rest (for 2 minutes) and try again with a heavier weight. If they fail, they rest and try again with a lighter weight.
3) The heaviest weight the performer can lift is their one rep max (1RM).
4) The results are compared to values in a published data table.

You can also estimate your 1RM using online calculators, which is a safer method.

Reliability

1) The performer may get tired if they lift too many weights before finding their 1RM.
2) This means they don't get an accurate value of their 1RM.

Validity

1) The test only measures the muscular strength of the muscle groups you are targeting, e.g. leg strength.
2) This means it is not a valid test for testing the strength of other muscle groups.

My favourite machine to use at the gym is the vending machine...

It's essential to perform the one rep max test safely — the performer needs to start with an appropriate weight (not something ridiculously heavy) and have a spotter who can assist them if they struggle.

Body Composition Tests

This page gives you a few examples of tests that can be used to measure a performer's body composition.

Body Mass Index (BMI) Estimates Ideal Weight

BMI — Standard procedure

Equipment: weighing scales, tape measure.

1) The sports performer's body mass (weight) is measured using scales, in kilograms (kg).
2) Their height is measured using a tape measure, in metres (m).
3) Their body mass index (BMI) is calculated using this formula:
4) The results of this test are given in kg/m² and compared to values in a published data table.

$$BMI = \frac{body\ mass\ (kg)}{height^2\ (m^2)}$$

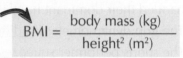

height² = height × height

Reliability

If height and weight are not measured accurately the results will be unreliable.

Validity

1) People with more muscle, e.g. sprinters, have a higher body mass. This makes the test less valid.
2) Pregnant women carry more weight due to the baby. This means the test is not valid for pregnant women.

Bioelectrical Impedance Analysis (BIA) Uses Electrical Currents

BIA — Standard procedure

Equipment: BIA device, mat.

1) The sports performer lays down on a mat and electrodes are attached to the right ankle and right wrist.
2) A small electrical current passes through the body.
3) The BIA device gives out a reading, adjusted for the performer's height and weight — this is the estimated percentage (%) body fat.
4) The result is compared to values in a published data table.

Reliability

If the sports performer drinks more or less water than normal this can affect the results.

Waist to Hip Ratio Gives an Idea of Body Fat

Waist to Hip Ratio — Standard procedure

Equipment: tape measure.

1) Measure around the smallest part of a performer's waist and the widest part of the hips using a tape measure.
2) Divide the waist measurement by the hips measurement to find a ratio.
3) The result is compared to values in a published data table.

I ate a shocking cake the other day — it had electrical currants in it...

The tests on this page give estimates for body composition — they give an idea of how much of your body is made up of fat. Although they are just estimates, they are still useful for tracking fitness over time.

Agility Tests

This section looks at tests for skill-related fitness. The tests below will measure your agility.

The Illinois Agility Run Test and T-Test are Agility Courses

Illinois Agility Run Test — Standard procedure

Equipment: cones, tape measure, stopwatch.

1) Set up the course as shown on the right.
2) The sports performer starts by lying face down with their head level with the start line.

start line ➡

3) On the word 'GO', they get up and run the course as fast as they can.
4) Another person uses a stopwatch to time how long it takes them to finish the course.
5) The results of this test are given in seconds.
6) The results are compared to values in a published data table.

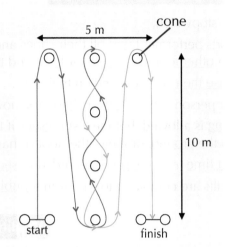

T-Test — Standard procedure

Equipment: cones, tape measure, stopwatch.

1) Set up the course as shown on the right.
2) The sports performer stands ready at the start cone.
3) On the word 'GO', the performer must:
   - Run forwards to Cone A and touch it with the right hand.
   - Sidestep to Cone B and touch it with the left hand.
   - Sidestep to Cone C and touch it with the right hand.
   - Sidestep to Cone A and touch it with the left hand.
   - Run backwards to the start cone.
4) Another person uses a stopwatch to time how long it takes them to finish the course.
5) The results of this test are given in seconds.
6) The results are compared to values in a published data table.

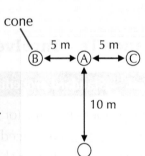

Reliability

1) A change in the weather can affect the results of both tests — it's easy to slip over in wet conditions.
2) If the sports performer is not wearing the right footwear they might be slower. This can make the results less reliable.

Validity

1) Both tests are valid tests of agility for sports that involve running.
2) They're less valid for sports that don't involve running. For example, kayaking.

The T-test is in the running to be my favourite fitness test...

Both of these agility tests use the same equipment but the courses are very different. Performers only run forwards during the Illinois agility run test, but must run forwards, backwards and sideways for the T-test.

Balance Tests

Balance is another component of fitness you can measure. Here are two tests you need to know.

You Balance on One Leg in the Stork Stand Test

Stork Stand Test — Standard procedure

Equipment: stopwatch.

1) The sports performer takes off their shoes and stands on their best leg with the other foot touching their knee and their hands on their hips.
2) They raise their heel to stand on their toes.
3) Another person uses a stopwatch to time how long they can hold the position for.
4) Wobbling is allowed, but the test finishes if their heel touches the ground, or their other foot or hands move.
5) The best time in three tries is recorded in seconds.
6) The results are compared to values in a published data table.

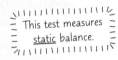
This test measures static balance.

Reliability

Some people might disagree with what does or doesn't count as failing the test. This means the results could be less reliable.

Validity

1) This test is a valid test in sports where you need to balance on the balls of your feet, e.g. ballet dancing.
2) It's less valid for sports where you don't need to balance on your feet, e.g. horse riding.

The Y Balance Test Involves Stretching in Three Directions

Y Balance Test — Standard procedure

Equipment: tape measure, tape (or specialist Y balance test equipment).

1) Three pieces of tape are placed on the floor to create a Y shape.
2) The performer takes off their shoes and stands on one foot at the centre of the Y.
3) They stretch their free leg to one point of the Y as far as they can. They can bend their standing knee to reach further.
4) They repeat this three times on the same leg for each point on the Y, always facing the same direction. Then, they repeat it on the other leg.
5) Another person measures each attempt. If part of the performer touches the floor (apart from the foot of the free leg) the result doesn't count.
6) The average distances in each direction are recorded and the results are compared to values in a published data table.

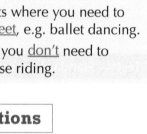
This equipment has boxes that you slide along with the feet.

A

stand here, facing A

90°

Reliability

Results are more reliable using the Y balance test equipment, rather than with a tape measure and tape.

Validity

1) This test is a valid test in sports where you need to do dynamic balances on the feet.
2) It is less valid for sports requiring static balances or upper body balances.

Y balance? Well, it's a useful skill for some sports...

The stork stand test is useful for testing static balance, whereas the Y balance test is better for testing dynamic balance. Think of your own examples of sports that would benefit from each type of balance.

Coordination Tests

Next up is <u>coordination</u> and another two tests for you to learn.

The **Wall-Toss Test** Measures your **Hand-Eye Coordination**

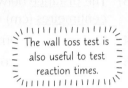

Hand-eye coordination is the ability of your hands and eyes to work together to do things.

The <u>Alternate-Hand Wall-Toss Test</u> is also called the <u>Wall Toss Test</u> or <u>Wall Throw Test</u>.

Alternate-Hand Wall-Toss Test — Standard procedure

Equipment: tennis ball, wall, stopwatch.
1) The sports performer starts by standing 2 m away from a <u>smooth wall</u>.
2) They <u>throw</u> a ball underarm using their <u>right</u> hand against the wall and catch it in their <u>left</u> hand.
3) They then throw it underarm using their <u>left</u> hand and catch it in their <u>right</u> hand.
4) They repeat this for <u>30 seconds</u> and count the <u>number of catches</u>.
5) The <u>more</u> successful catches they make, the <u>better</u> their <u>coordination</u>.
6) The results are compared to values in a <u>published data table</u>.

The wall toss test is also useful to test reaction times.

Reliability

1) The test should be repeated using the <u>same ball</u> and <u>same wall</u>.
2) The results <u>won't</u> be as reliable if these <u>conditions</u> are <u>not</u> the same.

Validity

The test is <u>less valid</u> for sports that <u>don't</u> use the hands, e.g. <u>skateboarding</u> or <u>football</u>.

I didn't say *kick* flip...

You **Flip and Catch Sticks** in the **Stick Flip Test**

Stick Flip Coordination Test — Standard procedure

Equipment: 3 sticks (60 cm long and 2 cm thick), one with tape at one end.
1) The sports performer holds <u>one stick in each hand</u>, and <u>rests</u> the <u>taped stick</u> on the two sticks.
2) They try <u>5 half-flips</u> — one hand flicks the <u>taped stick</u> so it does a <u>half-rotation</u> and lands back on the <u>two sticks</u>. The <u>taped end</u> lands on the <u>other side</u>.
3) They try <u>5 full-flips</u> — the taped stick does a <u>full rotation</u>. The taped end lands on the <u>same side</u>.
4) The flip <u>fails</u> if the stick <u>falls to the ground</u> or <u>doesn't</u> do the <u>correct rotation</u>.
5) After all <u>10 attempts</u>, the performer is scored — they get <u>1 point</u> for each successful <u>half-flip</u> and <u>2 points</u> for each successful <u>full-flip</u>. The <u>maximum</u> they can score is <u>15 points</u>.
6) The results are compared to values in a <u>published data table</u>.

Reliability

1) Having sticks that are too <u>light</u> or <u>heavy</u> could make the test <u>more challenging</u> or <u>too easy</u>.
2) This makes the results <u>less reliable</u>.

Validity

As above, the test is <u>less valid</u> for sports that <u>don't</u> use the <u>same</u> types of <u>hand movements</u>.

Want to improve your coordination? You've got to stick at it...

It can be easier to remember the equipment needed, set-up and procedure of a fitness test if you carry it out <u>yourself</u> — have a go at running one of these coordination tests with a partner.

Power Tests

These tests all measure a performer's power.

Jumping Tests are a Good Way to Measure Leg Power

Vertical Jump Test — Standard procedure

Equipment: wall, chalk, tape measure.

1) The sports performer reaches as high as they can
   (with feet flat on the floor) and makes a chalk mark on a wall.
2) Next, they jump up as high as they can.
   They make another chalk mark.
3) The distance between the chalk is measured in
   centimetres (cm) with a tape measure.
4) The sports performer gets three turns. Their best score is recorded.
5) The results are compared to values in a published data table.

Standing Long Jump — Standard procedure

Equipment: tape, tape measure.

1) The sports performer stands behind a line of tape.
2) They jump two-footed as far as they can, bending their
   knees and swinging their arms to push them forward.
3) The distance between the tape and where the back of the performer's
   heels landed is measured in centimetres (cm) with a tape measure.
4) The sports performer gets three turns. Their best score is recorded.
5) The results are compared to values in a published data table.

Margaria-Kalamen Power Test — Standard procedure

Equipment: tape measure, tape, weighing scales, stopwatch, cones, stairs/steps.

1) The sports performer's body mass (weight) is measured using scales, in kilograms (kg).
2) Cones are placed on the 3rd, 6th and 9th steps and tape is placed 6 metres before the steps.
3) The vertical distance is measured, in metres, between the 3rd and 9th steps.
4) The performer starts at the tape and runs towards and up the steps,
   jumping only on the steps marked with cones (3rd, 6th and 9th steps).
5) Another person measures the time, in seconds, to get from the 3rd step to the 9th step.
6) Power, in watts,
   is worked out
   using a formula:

This test has no table to compare results against.

$$\text{Power (W)} = \text{body mass (kg)} \times \text{vertical distance (m)} \times \frac{9.8}{\text{time taken (s)}}$$

Reliability

1) A bad jumping technique can lead
   to a lower score on each test.
2) This makes the results less reliable.

Validity

1) These tests measure power of the leg muscles.
2) This means they are not valid tests for
   testing the power of other muscle groups.

Revise more I tell you — sorry, all this power's gone to my head...

The Margaria-Kalamen power test has a more complicated set-up than the other power tests —
if you're using the stairway of a building, make sure to close it off to others to avoid any accidents.

Reaction Time Tests

You've made it — this is the final page on the fitness tests that you need to know.
These tests are used to measure the reaction time of a performer.

A Performer Catches a Ruler in the Ruler Drop Test

Ruler Drop Test — Standard procedure

Equipment: ruler.

1) The person running the test holds the ruler out vertically.

2) The sports performer lightly places their first finger on the ruler, so that the 0 cm mark on the ruler is in line with the top of the finger.

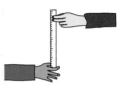

3) The ruler is dropped without warning and the performer must catch it as quickly as they can.

4) The measurement on the ruler at the point where it was caught is how far the ruler dropped in the time it took the performer to react.

5) The longer the distance, the longer the reaction time.

6) The sports performer gets three turns. Their average score is taken as the result.

7) The results are compared to values in a published data table.

Reliability

1) If a performer is tired, reaction times can be slower than usual.

2) Caffeine (e.g. in coffee) may also affect reaction times, making results less reliable.

Validity

The test only uses a performer's hands, but many sports require performers to react with different parts of the body (e.g. a sprinter leaving the blocks).

You can Go Online to Test your Reaction Time

1) Online reaction time tests are simple ways of testing a performer's reaction time.

2) There are many different websites and apps that are available.

3) Performers must respond to a stimulus (e.g. a changing colour, flashing light or noise) and click or tap as quickly as possible.

4) The computer records the time taken to respond — it will be a more accurate measure than someone using a stopwatch.

5) The results can be compared with other people that use the same website or app.

Take me to your ruler...

The ruler drop test uses a visual stimulus to test reaction times. Online reaction time tests can use sound as a stimulus, which may be a more valid test for athletes that react to a starting gun, e.g. sprinters.

Fitness Test Results

You need to be able to interpret data from a fitness test to help you evaluate and plan fitness training.

Coaches can Compare Results to Normative Data

1) A coach needs to interpret (work out the meaning of) fitness test results.
2) This helps them to make a performer's training programme better.
3) One way of interpreting results is to compare them to published data tables.
4) These tables show normative data — this is average or 'normal' data that has been collected from a large number of people who have completed the fitness test.
5) Most fitness tests have data tables for specific groups, e.g. males / females of a certain age group.

When you compare results to normative data, you are analysing data.

EXAMPLE

The published data table below is for 16- to 19-year-olds taking the grip dynamometer test. Find the rating for an 18-year-old female performer who scored 26 kg.

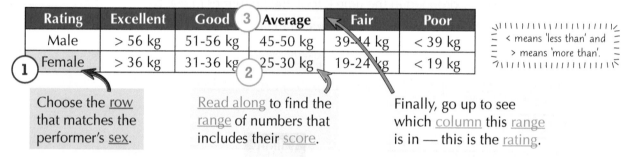

Rating	Excellent	Good	Average	Fair	Poor
Male	> 56 kg	51-56 kg	45-50 kg	39-44 kg	< 39 kg
Female	> 36 kg	31-36 kg	25-30 kg	19-24 kg	< 19 kg

< means 'less than' and > means 'more than'.

① Choose the row that matches the performer's sex.

② Read along to find the range of numbers that includes their score.

Finally, go up to see which column this range is in — this is the rating.

So, this performer has average grip strength for her age and sex.

Coaches Use Data to Suggest Fitness Improvements

1) You can recommend changes to a training programme after analysing data from fitness tests.
2) For example, a performer has an excellent rating for flexibility and a poor rating for speed. Their training programme probably won't need more flexibility training, but will need more activities designed to improve speed.
3) You can measure the effect of training by doing regular fitness tests and comparing data over time.

EXAMPLE

Bryan's training programme aims to improve his aerobic endurance and muscular endurance.

Fitness Test	Week 1	2	3	4	5
12-Minute Cooper Run (distance in m)	1450	1490	1530	1600	1640
1-Minute Sit-Up Test (no. of sit-ups)	45	46	45	46	44

Bryan improves his score on the 12-Minute Cooper Run each week. This shows his aerobic endurance is improving.

Bryan does about the same number of sit-ups each week, so his abdominal muscular endurance is not improving. His training programme should change to improve his muscular endurance.

I'd rate myself 'excellent' thank you very much...

In the exam, you might need to interpret fitness results, e.g. suggest the components of fitness a performer should work on given test ratings. Make sure your suggestions are appropriate for the performer's sport.

Fitness Training Methods

You need to know how to safely and effectively take part in fitness training. This includes linking the training principles to training methods. Flick back to pages 49 and 50 to see all the training principles.

Before Exercise You Should Always Warm Up...

1) It's important to do a warm-up before taking part in any fitness training.
2) A warm-up gets your body ready for exercise by gradually increasing your work rate. It also reduces the risk of injury.
3) A warm-up should include:

 A pulse raiser (see p.25)
- Light exercise that increases your heart rate, breathing rate and blood flow.
- It helps to ease your body into exercising by gradually increasing the exercise intensity, and it increases the oxygen supply to the muscles.

 A mobiliser (see p.26)
- Mobilisers are low-intensity exercises that take joints through their full range of motion.
- They reduce the heart rate and breathing rate slightly.
- They increase the production of synovial fluid, which increases lubrication of the joints.

③ **Stretches** (see p.26-27)
- The final stage stretches the muscles that will be used in the fitness training method.
- This can involve static and dynamic stretches.
- Stretching muscles makes them more pliable, so injuries are less likely.

...And Afterwards You Should Cool Down

1) A cool-down gets your body back to normal after exercise by gradually lowering your pulse and breathing rate to resting levels.
2) A cool-down should involve:

 Gentle exercise
- Gentle exercise like jogging is a great way to cool down.
- You should gradually reduce the intensity of this exercise so that your heart rate, breathing rate and body temperature return to normal.
- It also means you can continue taking in more oxygen to help get rid of lactic acid — a waste product that builds up during exercise.

② **Stretches**
- The muscles that have been used in the fitness training method should be stretched.
- This helps the muscles return to pre-exercise length.
- Static stretching while the muscles are warm helps to improve flexibility.

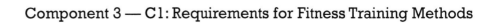

Fitness Training Methods

Training Methods Improve Components of Fitness

1) Fitness training methods are <u>different ways of exercising</u>.
2) Sports performers use these methods to improve <u>performance</u>.
3) Each method targets a different <u>component of fitness</u>.
4) For example, <u>continuous training</u> is a fitness training method for improving <u>aerobic endurance</u>.

See the next page for continuous training.

Coaches Apply Training Principles to Training Methods

1) Coaches design <u>training programmes</u> to help sports performers <u>improve</u> at their sport.
2) They <u>apply</u> the <u>basic training principles</u> and <u>additional training principles</u> to each training method.

EXAMPLE

Continuous Training — Cyclist (beginner)

Basic training principles (FITT):

- **Frequency** — <u>4 times per week</u>.
- **Intensity** — <u>moderate</u> (medium).
- **Time** — each session needs to be at least <u>30 minutes</u> long.
- **Type** — <u>continuous training</u>.

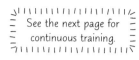
Reminder
Frequency — how often to train.
Intensity — how hard to train.
Time — how long to train for.
Type — which training method to use.

Additional training principles:

- **Progressive overload** — the intensity is <u>moderate</u> to match the <u>demands</u> of distance cycling, but should get <u>gradually harder</u> to <u>overload</u> the body.
- **Specificity** — the training improves <u>aerobic endurance</u>, which is important for cycling.
- **Individual differences/needs** — a <u>beginner</u> will have lower <u>fitness</u> and <u>skill</u> than an elite cyclist.
- **Adaptation** — the body will get <u>fitter</u> in the recovery between each session.
- **Reversibility** — fitness will <u>decrease</u> if training stops or the cyclist doesn't train hard enough.
- **Variation** — the cycling <u>route</u> can be varied to make it interesting.
- **Rest and recovery** — 3 days of <u>rest</u> per week will allow the body to recover.

Training Should Match the Required Intensity

Coaches decide on the exercise <u>intensity</u>, e.g. percentage of maximum heart rate (see p.53), depending on the performer's <u>fitness</u> and the chosen <u>training method</u>.

EXAMPLE

- For <u>aerobic endurance training</u>, the performer's <u>heart rate</u> needs to be in the <u>aerobic target zone</u> (60-80% of maximum heart rate).
- To achieve this, the exercise <u>intensity</u> should be <u>moderate</u>.

Putting on a big jumper — another great way to warm up...

You should warm up and cool down every time you take part in fitness training. It helps to prevent injuries to muscles (like strains) and makes sure that your heart rate and breathing rate gradually changes.

Aerobic Endurance Training

Aerobic endurance training is all about increasing how long you can keep exercising for.
The next two pages cover the four methods of training that you need to know.

Continuous Training Means No Resting

1) Continuous training is where you keep doing the same type of exercise without having a rest.
2) The exercise needs to last for 30 minutes or longer.
3) The intensity is moderate (medium). You keep going at the same steady pace.
4) It works well for sports such as running, cycling and swimming.

Advantages and Disadvantages:

Advantages:
- No specialist equipment or set-up is needed.
- Can be done almost anywhere, e.g. a park, sports hall or running track.
- Many people can take part at once.

Disadvantage:
- It can be boring doing one exercise at the same pace.

This is too intense...

Fartlek Training is All About Changes of Intensity

1) Fartlek training involves changes in intensity.
2) There are no rest periods when training.
3) You can change the intensity of the training by:
   - Using equipment such as weights or a weighted backpack.
   - Changing the speed — for example, by running fast for one part and slow for another part.
   - Changing the terrain (type of land), e.g. a flat road, hilly grass or soft sand.

Fartlek means 'speed play' in Swedish.

4) You can include a mix of aerobic and anaerobic activity, so it's good training for sports that need different paces, like hockey and rugby.

Advantages and Disadvantages:

Advantages:
- No specialist equipment or set-up is needed.
- It can be made easy or hard to match your fitness.
- Many people can take part at once.

Disadvantages:
- Changes to intensity means that there isn't a clear structure — it's easy to skip the hard bits.
- It's difficult to track progress.

Aerobic Endurance Training

Interval Training Uses Fixed Patterns of Exercise

1) Interval training is where you have a <u>work period</u> and then a <u>rest or recovery period</u>.
2) In the work period you exercise at <u>moderate intensity</u> for <u>30 seconds to five minutes</u>.
3) In the rest or recovery period you can <u>sit down</u>, <u>stand still</u>, <u>walk</u> or <u>jog</u>.
4) It is an ideal training method for people with <u>low fitness</u> because the performer can start with <u>short work periods</u> and <u>long rest periods</u>.
5) To <u>develop</u> aerobic endurance, you need to <u>decrease</u> the <u>number</u> or <u>length</u> of the <u>rest or recovery periods</u>.

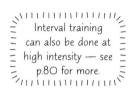
Interval training can also be done at high intensity — see p.80 for more.

Just one more rest period...

Advantages and Disadvantages:

Advantages:
- It can be <u>adapted</u> for all <u>fitness levels</u>.
- No <u>specialist equipment</u> or <u>set-up</u> is needed.
- <u>Many people</u> can take part at once.

Disadvantage:
- Rest periods can make it <u>time-consuming</u>.

Circuit Training Uses Loads of Different Exercises

1) In circuit training, you do <u>one exercise after another</u> in a <u>set order</u>.
2) Each exercise is called a 'station'. Circuits are <u>timed</u> or have a <u>set number</u> of exercises to complete at each station.
3) Only taking <u>short rests</u> between stations improves aerobic endurance.

EXAMPLE

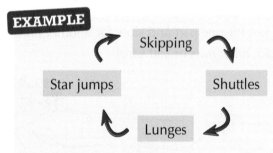

Skipping → Shuttles → Lunges → Star jumps →

- <u>Four stations</u>
- <u>30 seconds work</u> at each station.
- <u>30 seconds rest</u> between each station.
- Repeat the circuit <u>three times</u>.

Advantages and Disadvantages:

Advantages:
- You <u>design</u> the circuit, so you can match circuit training to an <u>individual</u>.
- The <u>variety</u> keeps training <u>interesting</u>.
- <u>Many people</u> can take part at once.

Disadvantage:
- It can take time to <u>set up</u> if lots of <u>equipment</u> is used.

I need some rest after that work period...

There were four main training methods for aerobic endurance for you there — make sure you know the advantages and disadvantages of each, and can list sports that benefit from these training methods.

Flexibility Training

Sports performers can improve their flexibility by training, which involves stretching alone or with a partner.

Static Stretching Can be Used to Improve Flexibility

1) Static stretching is when you gradually stretch a muscle and hold it in one position.
2) Static stretching can be active or passive.

- In an active static stretch, you hold the stretch position by yourself (you apply an internal force).
- In a passive static stretch, you use someone else or an object, such as a wall or a resistance band, to hold the stretch position (an external force is applied).

Advantages and Disadvantages:

Advantages:
- Anyone can do it, even with little previous training.
- No specialist equipment or set-up is needed.
- Many people can take part at once.

Disadvantages:
- Poor technique can lead to overstretching and injury.
- It is only effective for stretching certain muscle groups.

Stretching? No, I always sit like this.

Proprioceptive Neuromuscular Facilitation (PNF) Uses a Partner

1) Don't worry about all those long words — you can call this training method PNF.
2) It is best to use a partner to help you do this type of stretching:

You can use an immovable object instead of a partner, e.g. a wall. You push against the wall in step 2 and stretch a bit further by yourself in step 3.

1 The performer stretches the muscle as far as it can go.

2 A partner helps to hold the muscle and the performer pushes against them for 6-10s. The muscle is in an isometric contraction — it contracts but stays the same length.

3 The performer relaxes the muscle whilst the partner stretches it a little bit more.

3) Muscles have a stretch reflex that stops them being stretched too far.
4) PNF helps you push past the stretch reflex, meaning muscles can be stretched further than normal.

Advantages and Disadvantages:

Advantages:
- It develops flexibility more quickly than other methods.
- No specialist equipment or set-up is needed.

Disadvantages:
- It is not a suitable method for children.
- There is a greater risk of injury.

I'm stretching myself thin to find a good pun here...

It's important to remember the difference between the types of static stretching. You hold the stretch position yourself in an active static stretch, but you use an object or partner in a passive static stretch.

Muscular Endurance and Strength Training

Sports performers can make their <u>muscles stronger</u> by using <u>weights</u> and <u>body resistance exercises</u>.

Weight Training is Described in Numbers of Sets and Reps

1) Weight training is described in <u>reps</u> (repetitions) and <u>sets</u> (a group of reps without rest).
2) After each set it is important to have a <u>rest period</u> of about <u>1-2 minutes</u>.

EXAMPLE

A person might do <u>2 sets</u> of <u>6 reps</u>.

1st set  × 6 → 1-2 minutes rest → 2nd set  × 6 → 1-2 minutes rest

3) The <u>weight</u> and the <u>number of sets and reps</u> you should do will depend on whether you want to train <u>muscular endurance</u> or <u>muscular strength</u>:

- To increase <u>muscular endurance</u>, you use <u>low weight</u> (loads) but a <u>high number of reps</u>.
- To increase <u>muscular strength</u> you use <u>high weight</u> (loads) but a <u>low number of reps</u>.

4) <u>Free weights</u> and <u>fixed resistance machines</u> can be used for <u>muscular endurance training</u> or <u>muscular strength training</u>.

Free Weights are Not Attached to a Piece of Equipment

1) Free weights are weights that <u>aren't attached</u> to a machine. For example:

a barbell →     ← a dumbbell

2) You lift <u>barbells</u> with <u>both hands</u> and <u>dumbbells</u> with <u>one hand</u>.
3) Free weights can be used to target <u>specific muscle groups</u>, e.g.:

- <u>biceps curls</u> (dumbbells) target the <u>biceps</u>
- <u>bench presses</u> (barbells) target the <u>triceps</u>, <u>deltoids</u> and <u>chest muscles</u>
- <u>squats</u> (barbells) target the <u>quadriceps</u> and <u>gluteus maximus</u>

You can determine the amount of weight you should lift by doing RM tests — see p.55.

4) It's <u>important</u> to have a <u>spotter</u> for <u>heavy weights</u> to watch you and help you <u>lift safely</u>.

Advantages and Disadvantages:

Advantages:
- You can <u>target</u> the particular <u>muscles</u> that you want to improve.
- Smaller weights can be used <u>anywhere</u>, e.g. at home.

Disadvantages:
- You need to choose a <u>correct weight</u> and use a <u>good technique</u> or you can <u>injure</u> your muscles.
- The <u>number of people</u> that can take part depends on the <u>equipment available</u>.
- Requires <u>specialist equipment</u> or <u>facilities</u>.
- <u>Heavy loads</u> are <u>not suitable</u> for <u>young children</u>.

Muscular Endurance and Strength Training

Fixed Resistance Machines Target Specific Muscles

1) Fixed resistance machines have weights attached to pulleys. You can change how heavy the weight is.

2) The direction you move the weight is fixed, which means each machine has a set exercise and muscle group that it targets.

3) E.g. the seated chest press targets the triceps, deltoids and chest muscles.

Advantages and Disadvantages:

Advantages:
- They're great for beginners, because muscle movement is controlled.
- They are easy to use, which reduces the risk of injury.

Disadvantages:
- They only exercise one muscle group.
- Only one person can exercise per machine.
- Requires specialist equipment or facilities which can be expensive.

Circuit Training Can Develop Muscular Endurance

1) Circuit training (see p.76) can be used to increase muscular endurance.

2) The circuit stations can each target different muscles. This means the muscles don't get fatigued (too tired).

squats

calf raises

biceps curls

sit-ups

lunges

This circuit involves free weights and body resistance exercises, e.g. sit-ups.

Advantages and Disadvantages:

Advantages:
- They are varied and can be changed to make exercise more interesting.
- They exercise the whole body.
- Many people can take part at once.

Disadvantages:
- It can take time to set up if lots of equipment is used.
- Some circuits need specialist equipment.

I prefer wait training myself — far less strenuous...

Make sure you understand how weights can help improve muscular endurance or muscular strength. For endurance, do low weight, high reps. For strength, do high weight, low reps. It's that simple.

Speed Training

Speed training involves going as <u>fast as you can</u> for a short distance and then having lots of <u>rest</u>.

Acceleration Sprints Gradually Increase the Pace

1) In acceleration sprints you keep <u>increasing the pace</u> over a <u>short distance</u>.
2) You start <u>standing still</u> or <u>rolling</u> (easy jogging), then increase the pace to <u>jogging</u>, then <u>striding</u> and then to a <u>maximal sprint</u>.
3) In between each sprint you <u>rest</u> by <u>jogging</u> or <u>walking</u>.

Advantages and Disadvantages:

Advantages:
- <u>Gradually</u> increasing the pace <u>reduces</u> the risk of <u>injury</u>.
- No <u>specialist equipment</u> or <u>set-up</u> is needed.
- <u>Many people</u> can take part at once.

Disadvantage:
- Not suitable for sports where acceleration <u>isn't gradual</u>, e.g. <u>sprinting</u>.

Interval Training Uses Fixed Patterns of Exercise

1) Interval training (see p.76) can be <u>adapted</u> for <u>anaerobic exercise</u>, e.g. <u>sprinting</u>.
2) To develop <u>speed</u>, the <u>work period</u> needs to be at a <u>higher intensity</u>.
3) However, you should also <u>increase</u> the <u>number</u> or <u>length</u> of the <u>rest periods</u>.

Advantages and Disadvantages:

Advantages:
- It can be <u>easily adapted</u> to suit an individual.
- No <u>specialist equipment</u> or <u>set-up</u> is needed.
- <u>Many people</u> can take part at once.

Disadvantage:
- There is a higher risk of <u>injury</u>, as the intensity is higher.

Add Resistance to Increase the Difficulty

1) <u>Resistance drills</u> involve sprinting with <u>resistance</u>.
2) The <u>terrain</u> can provide resistance, e.g. running <u>uphill</u>.
3) Or <u>equipment</u> can be used to <u>hold back</u> a performer as they run, e.g. <u>parachutes</u>, <u>sleds</u>, <u>bungee ropes</u> and <u>resistance bands</u>.

Advantages and Disadvantages:

Advantages:
- Variety makes this method more <u>interesting</u>.
- It also improves <u>muscular strength</u>.

Disadvantages:
- If loads are too heavy, there is a risk of <u>injury</u>.
- Some equipment can be <u>expensive</u>.
- The <u>number of people</u> that can take part depends on the <u>equipment available</u>.

Don't resist learning this page — you know you want to...

Speed training is useful for many sports that involve sprinting in straight lines, e.g. in football or hockey to intercept a ball. But these sports also require changes in direction, which is where agility comes in...

Agility and Power Training

SAQ training helps to develop a sports performer's agility, and plyometrics makes you powerful.

SAQ Training Involves Speed, Agility and Quickness

1) Sports performers use Speed, Agility and Quickness training (SAQ) to develop their motor skills (muscle movements). It helps them practise moving quickly and changing direction.

2) In SAQ training, performers sprint and use agility to avoid obstacles (e.g. cones, ladders and posts). For example, a footballer may dribble around cones to practise avoiding opponents in a match.

3) SAQ training is helpful for sports that involve lots of quick movement, e.g. basketball and skiing.

Advantages and Disadvantages:

Advantages:
- It can be adapted to suit different sports.
- You do need some equipment, but it's not very expensive.
- Many people can take part at once.

Disadvantages:
- It can take time to set up if lots of equipment is used.
- You need to be fit — there is risk of injury if poor technique is used.

Plyometric Training Improves Power

1) Plyometrics develops explosive (sudden bursts of) power and muscular strength.

2) In the exercises the muscles lengthen and then quickly shorten, creating power.

3) The quicker the muscle shortens after lengthening, the more power is created.

4) Plyometrics is used by sprinters and hurdlers as well as netball, volleyball and basketball players.

5) Examples of plyometric exercises are: lunging, bounding, incline press-ups, barrier hopping and jumping.

6) It requires high levels of fitness.

EXAMPLE

Depth jumps increase how high you can jump. You drop off a box then quickly jump into the air. The first stage (as you land) lengthens your quadriceps and the second stage shortens them.

Advantages and Disadvantages:

Advantages:
- It can be adapted to develop specific muscle groups.
- You need some equipment (e.g. boxes or benches), but it's not very expensive.

Disadvantages:
- You need to be very fit to do it. Beginners, children and older adults shouldn't take part.
- The number of people that can take part depends on the equipment available.

What happened to the coach who overslept? They got the SAQ...

Both SAQ training and plyometric training require high levels of fitness and skill, so they're not suitable for everyone. Sports performers need a good technique and warm-up beforehand to avoid getting injured.

More Training Methods

There are a few more training methods to learn: balance, coordination and reaction time.

Balance Training Improves Posture and Strength

Balances can be static or dynamic (see p.35).

1) Balance training involves balancing on a limited base of support.
2) This helps to strengthen your core muscles and improve your posture.
3) It benefits performers across different sports by developing control and stability. It can also help to prevent injuries.
4) An example is raising your arm and opposite leg on a mat.

Advantages and Disadvantages:

Advantages:
- It's suitable for all age groups and abilities.
- No specialist equipment or set-up is needed.
- Many people can take part at once.

Disadvantage:
- There is a risk of falling, particularly for older adults.

Coordination Training Uses Two or More Body Parts

1) Coordination training involves moving two or more body parts at the same time.
2) It improves the sports performer's ability to move smoothly.
3) Examples include using a skipping rope or replicating the same movements as the sport, e.g. repeatedly hitting a table tennis ball (hand-eye coordination).

Advantages and Disadvantages:

Advantages:
- It can be adapted for any sport.
- Many people can take part at once, depending on the activity.

Disadvantages:
- It requires concentration to perform well.
- You may need specialist equipment and time to set up, depending on the activity.

Reaction Time Training Helps You Develop Quick Responses

1) Reaction time training makes you quicker at responding to external stimuli.
2) It's helpful for sprinters and players of racket sports (e.g. responding to the opponent hitting a ball).
3) For example, a sports performer could practise sprinting after the sound of a whistle.

Advantages and Disadvantages:

Advantages:
- No specialist equipment or set-up is needed for some activities.
- Many people can take part at once, depending on the activity.

Disadvantages:
- You often need a partner to help you to provide the stimuli.
- Some equipment is expensive, e.g. machines that fire tennis balls.

I can sip my tea and change the channel at the same time...

Remember, a sports performer must keep their centre of mass over their base of support to balance well. If you make the base of support smaller in balance training, it'll make it more difficult for the performer.

Choosing Training Methods

There are different <u>factors</u> to consider when choosing a training method for a participant.

Think About the Demands of the Sport...

This is linked to the training principle of 'specificity'.

1) Firstly, think about the <u>area</u> of the sport or physical activity you want to <u>improve</u>, including the <u>components of fitness</u> that are involved, and which <u>parts of the body</u> too.

2) Plan how you can <u>recreate</u> the <u>demands</u> of the sport or physical activity, e.g. using the same <u>equipment</u> and <u>conditions</u> as a <u>competitive environment</u>.

...and the Practical Considerations

Then, you should think about the <u>practical factors</u> involved:

I'm rich!

Cost of equipment

Some training methods need <u>specialist equipment</u>, such as <u>fixed resistance machines</u>, which can be <u>expensive</u> to buy. You may have to <u>hire</u> equipment instead.

Location of training

Some training methods need a <u>specific facility</u>, such as a <u>swimming pool</u> or <u>gym</u>.
Participants will need to <u>travel</u> to these facilities, and they will only be <u>open</u> at <u>certain times</u> of day.

Ease of set-up

Some training methods involve <u>setting up</u>, e.g. <u>circuit training</u>, which can take <u>time</u>.
<u>Equipment</u> must be <u>stored</u> somewhere <u>between</u> sessions too.

Number of participants

Participants of <u>team sports</u> often <u>train together</u>. If you have <u>limited equipment</u>, you'll need to make smaller groups to share equipment.
The number of participants you can train will also be <u>limited</u> by the <u>amount of space</u> that you have access to.

Adapt Training to Meet the Participant's Needs

You'll also need to consider the <u>needs</u> of the participant, including:

* **Age** — <u>children</u> should avoid lifting <u>heavy weights</u>, e.g. in <u>muscular strength</u> training, as it can affect their <u>growth</u>. <u>High-intensity</u> activities, e.g. <u>resistance drills</u>, are not appropriate for <u>older adults</u>.

* **Level of fitness / experience** — training methods such as <u>plyometrics</u> are <u>too demanding</u> for people with <u>low fitness</u>. Training methods that can be <u>easily adapted</u>, e.g. <u>interval training</u>, can be more appropriate for <u>beginners</u>.

* **Variety** — the <u>training method</u> should be <u>interesting</u> for the participant. For example, <u>circuit training</u> is <u>varied</u>, so can be more <u>engaging</u> for <u>adolescents</u>.

Training with other people can also be more motivating.

I'm tired after all that brain training...

Remember to consider the safety of the participant when you're choosing a fitness training method.
You need to make sure the method is safe and that you've taken into account their current fitness level.

Provision of Fitness Training

You've already covered <u>provision</u> on pages 6-7, so this page should feel familiar...
but it's important to consider how provision relates to <u>fitness training</u>.

There are Different Providers of Fitness Training

Public Provision

Public sector provision includes facilities or sessions run by <u>schools</u> or
<u>local authorities</u>, e.g. a <u>leisure centre</u> or an <u>outdoor gym</u> in a <u>public</u> park.

Advantages and Disadvantages:

Advantages:
- A <u>wide range</u> of training and equipment is usually available.
- Facilities are open to <u>everyone</u> in a local community.
- Sessions are usually <u>cheaper</u> than those from private providers.

Disadvantages:
- <u>Equipment</u> and <u>facilities</u> can be <u>limited</u> or <u>dated</u>.
- Sometimes you have to <u>pay</u> to hire equipment.
- There may not be access to <u>sports sector professionals</u> for support, e.g. personal trainers.

Private Provision

Private provision includes profit-making <u>individuals</u> or <u>companies</u>, e.g. a <u>personal trainer</u> or <u>private gym</u>.

Advantages and Disadvantages:

Advantages:
- A <u>wide range</u> of training and equipment is usually available.
- <u>Modern facilities</u> and <u>equipment</u> are provided.
- <u>Sports sector professionals</u> are usually available to support with training.

Disadvantages:
- It is <u>more expensive</u> than public provision — you usually pay a <u>membership fee</u>.
- Facilities and training are only available where there is <u>demand</u>.

Voluntary Provision

Voluntary provision includes clubs and events run by <u>volunteers</u>, e.g. a <u>local park run</u>.

Advantages and Disadvantages:

Advantages:
- Training is open to <u>everyone</u>.
- It's usually <u>cheap</u> to take part.
- <u>Facilities</u> are usually <u>hired</u> from the <u>public sector</u>, so there is a <u>wide range</u> of training and equipment.

Disadvantages:
- Participants usually have to <u>pay fees</u> to <u>cover costs</u> of facilities.
- Relies on <u>volunteers</u> and <u>money</u> from <u>sponsorship</u> and <u>fundraising</u>.

I don't write these jokes for the money — I do it for the love, man...

Some methods of training may be more suited to a certain type of provision. For example, beginners might
prefer to do weight training at a private gym because there is greater access to fixed resistance machines.

Long-Term Effects of Training

Training over a long period of time affects the different systems in your body.
See p.23-24 if you need a reminder on the cardiorespiratory and musculoskeletal systems.

Aerobic Endurance Training Improves the Cardiorespiratory System

Aerobic endurance training (see p.75-76) affects the cardiovascular system...

Cardiac Hypertrophy

1) Your heart is a muscle — when you exercise, it adapts and gets bigger and stronger.
   This is called cardiac hypertrophy.

2) A bigger, stronger heart will contract more strongly and have a
   larger stroke volume (it can pump more blood with each beat).

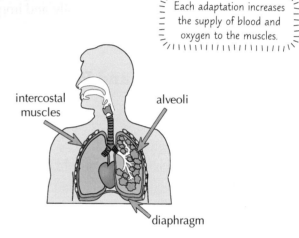

Boring trophy   Hypertrophy

Decreased Resting Heart Rate

1) As stroke volume increases, the heart has to beat less often
   to pump the same amount of blood around your body.

2) This means that your resting heart rate decreases.

...and also the respiratory system.

Each adaptation increases the supply of blood and oxygen to the muscles.

Increased Strength of Respiratory Muscles

1) Your diaphragm and intercostal muscles
   (the muscles between the ribs) get stronger.

2) This improves the efficiency of your breathing
   — it helps you get more air in and out of your
   body per breath, so more oxygen can be used
   by the working muscles whilst exercising.

intercostal muscles   alveoli

diaphragm

Increased Capillarisation Around Alveoli

1) Aerobic endurance training creates new capillaries (small blood vessels)
   at the alveoli ('air sacs' with thin walls) in the lungs.

2) This increases the rate of gaseous exchange — more oxygen can get into
   your bloodstream and more carbon dioxide can be removed (breathed out).

Flexibility Training Affects the Musculoskeletal System

Flexibility training causes these adaptations to the musculoskeletal system:

There is more production of synovial fluid in synovial joints,
which lubricates ('oils') joints and keeps them moving smoothly.

See p.23 for more on synovial joints.

There is an increase in the flexibility of ligaments and tendons.

There is an increase in the length of muscle fibres.

These adaptations all increase the range of movement permitted at joints.

Long-Term Effects of Training

Muscular Endurance Training Changes the Muscular System

Increased Capillarisation Around Muscle Tissues

1) Muscular endurance training increases the number of capillaries around the muscles.
2) Capillaries transfer blood containing oxygen and nutrients to the muscles so that they can release energy to keep contracting.
3) They also remove waste products.
4) A higher number of capillaries means more oxygen and nutrients can be supplied to the muscles and waste products can be removed more quickly.

Increased Muscle Tone

1) Muscle tone means how much tension there is in our muscles.
2) It keeps our body upright and stable.
3) Muscular endurance training increases muscle tone, which allows you to balance more easily and improves your posture.

Muscular Strength and Power Training Have Similar Effects

Muscle Hypertrophy

1) Muscular strength training makes your muscles thicker (hypertrophy).
2) As the muscles contract, small tears are created in the muscle fibres.
3) When these tears heal, the muscle tissue becomes bigger and stronger.

Increased Bone Density

1) The denser your bones, the stronger they are.
2) Muscular strength and power training put stress on your bones, causing the body to strengthen them by adding minerals.
3) The stronger your bones, the less likely they are to fracture.

Increased Tendon and Ligament Strength

1) Strength and power training both increase the strength of ligaments and tendons.
2) This means they are less likely to tear when you exercise, which helps avoid injury.

Speed Training also Affects the Muscular System

Increased Tolerance to Lactic Acid

1) Speed training uses lots of energy in a short space of time.
2) This creates lactic acid, which makes the muscles tired.
3) Long-term speed training makes the muscles more tolerant to lactic acid, so you can train more often and at a higher intensity without getting fatigued.

My brainular system feels like it's adapting...

It's important to learn how each of these changes to the body affect performance. Some adaptations may be useful for specific sports — for example, increased tolerance to lactic acid is really helpful for sprinting.

Fitness Programmes

A <u>fitness programme</u> is an <u>organised plan</u> to help improve a performer's fitness.

Fitness Programmes **Help to Achieve Aims**

1) <u>Sports performers</u> will have <u>goals</u> or <u>aims</u> that they want to <u>achieve</u> in their sport.

2) A <u>fitness programme</u> should also include <u>objectives</u> — these are the things that performers <u>need to do</u> to achieve their aims.

3) Objectives include the <u>components of fitness</u> to improve and the <u>methods of training</u> to use.

> **EXAMPLE**
>
> Terry — basketball player
>
> **Aim**: to improve at lay-up shots.
>
> **Objectives**:
>
> - <u>improve agility</u> (to help <u>move past defenders</u> quickly) using <u>SAQ training</u> (see p.81).
> - <u>improve power</u> (to help <u>jump high</u> and put the ball in the basket) using <u>plyometrics</u> (see p.81).

You'll Need to Collect **Personal Information**

Personal information should be stored securely and never shared with others.

1) You need <u>personal information</u> about a performer to make a fitness programme <u>suitable for their needs</u>.

2) Collecting the information might involve an <u>interview</u> and <u>questionnaires</u>, including a <u>PAR-Q</u> (see p.57), to check <u>current fitness</u> and <u>activity levels</u>.

3) <u>Health conditions</u>, <u>injuries</u> and <u>physical activity history</u> will <u>affect</u> the types of activity a performer can do.

4) <u>Lifestyle factors</u> (ways people <u>choose</u> to live their life) will also have an <u>effect</u>. E.g. if someone is a <u>heavy smoker</u> or <u>sedentary</u> (very inactive), their <u>ability</u> to carry out a <u>fitness programme</u> may be affected.

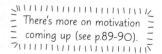

What? I exercise all the time...

Performers have a Level of **Motivation**

1) Performers will have a certain <u>attitude</u> (<u>feeling</u>) towards a fitness programme. This can be <u>determined</u> as part of the interview or questionnaire.

2) A performer needs a <u>positive attitude</u> to achieve <u>success</u>.

3) A fitness programme should also be <u>motivating</u> for a performer:

- If a performer takes part in activities they <u>enjoy</u> and they <u>feel progress</u>, they will have <u>high motivation</u>, and will want to <u>train hard</u> and <u>complete the programme</u>.
- However, if a programme is <u>too hard</u> (or <u>too easy</u>) for a performer, or they are <u>worried</u> about an <u>injury</u> or a <u>long-term health condition</u>, they will have <u>low motivation</u> and be more likely to <u>quit</u>.

There's more on motivation coming up (see p.89-90).

Archers seem to always be adjusting their aim...

One of the first steps with a fitness programme is deciding exactly what the performer is wanting to achieve — that may be improving a specific skill in a sport or a component of fitness (e.g. flexibility).

Fitness Programme Design

So you've collected personal information — now to <u>design</u> an <u>appropriate programme</u> for the performer.

Fitness Programmes should be Suited to the Performer

Follow these <u>steps</u> to <u>design</u> an effective <u>fitness programme</u>:

(1) <u>Collect personal information</u> and discuss a performer's <u>aims</u> (p.87).

(2) Carry out appropriate <u>fitness tests</u> to get a <u>baseline fitness level</u> (p.56-71).

(3) Identify <u>components of fitness</u> that need <u>improving</u> or <u>maintaining</u> (p.72) to meet the performer's aims.

(4) Select <u>appropriate training methods</u> (p.75-82), and apply the <u>principles of training</u> (p.49-50).

EXAMPLE

(1) **Name**: Terry   **Age**: 30   **Sex**: Male
Aim: to improve at lay-up shots.

PAR-Q [✔]   Pre-fitness checks [✔]

(2)

Fitness Test	Component of Fitness	Rating
T-test	Agility	Good
Vertical Jump Test	Power	Poor

(3) His programme should include <u>agility training</u> to improve his '<u>Good</u>' rating...

...but should include <u>more</u> activities to <u>train power</u>, as this component was '<u>Poor</u>'.

(4)

	Mon	Tue	Wed	Thu	Fri	Sat	Sun
Week 1	Plyometrics (85% MHR, 20 minutes)	*Rest*	SAQ training (30 minutes)	*Rest*	*Rest*	Plyometrics (85% MHR, 20 minutes)	*Rest*
Week 2	*Rest*	SAQ training (30 minutes)	*Rest*	Plyometrics (85% MHR, 20 minutes)	SAQ training (35 minutes)	*Rest*	Plyometrics (90% MHR, 20 minutes)

This fitness training programme applies <u>FITT principles</u>:
- <u>Frequency</u>: there are <u>3-5 training sessions</u> per <u>week</u>.
- <u>Intensity</u>: a <u>training target zone</u> is given for <u>plyometrics</u> training.
- <u>Time</u>: the <u>length</u> of each <u>session</u> is given.
- <u>Type</u>: SAQ training and plyometrics improve <u>agility</u> and <u>power</u>, which helps achieve his <u>aim</u>. <u>SAQ training</u> can be made <u>specific</u> to basketball, e.g. dribbling at speed around cones.

You can measure heart rate or estimate it using the Borg RPE scale (see p.52).

<u>Additional principles</u> of training are also applied, e.g.:
- <u>Rest and recovery</u>: there are <u>rest days</u> given each <u>week</u>.
- <u>Progressive overload</u>: there are <u>fewer rest days</u> in <u>week 2</u> and the <u>intensity increases over time</u>.

Designer fitness programme? Nah, a bit too expensive for me...

In the exam, you may be asked to evaluate a fitness programme. Think about whether the training methods are suitable for the performer in the question and if the training principles have been applied correctly.

Motivation and Goal Setting

Motivation is all about what <u>drives</u> you. It has lots of different <u>positive effects</u> on sports performers.

Motivation Makes You Want to Do Well

Motivation

> <u>Definition</u>: The <u>internal mechanisms</u> and <u>external stimuli</u> that <u>arouse</u> and <u>direct behaviour</u>.
> Or, in other words, the <u>factors</u> both <u>inside</u> and <u>outside</u> of you that make you <u>want</u> to <u>do something</u>.

1) <u>Motivation</u> is about how <u>keen</u> you are to do something.
   It's <u>what drives you</u>, particularly when things get difficult — your <u>desire</u> to <u>succeed</u>.

2) Motivation can be either <u>intrinsic</u> (from within yourself) or <u>extrinsic</u> (from outside).

Intrinsic Motivation

Motivation from <u>internal factors</u> — the <u>enjoyment</u> and good <u>feelings</u> you get from taking part in a sport or activity, e.g. <u>pride</u>, high <u>self-esteem</u>, enjoying the <u>challenge</u> or enjoying being part of a <u>team</u>.

Extrinsic Motivation

Motivation through <u>rewards</u> from other people/things. This can be <u>tangible</u> (you can <u>touch it</u>, e.g. trophies, money) or <u>intangible</u> (you <u>can't touch it</u>, e.g. applause, praise from a coach).

1) <u>Intrinsic motivation</u> is usually seen as the <u>most effective</u> — you're more likely to <u>train hard</u> and <u>finish</u> a training programme if you <u>enjoy it</u>.

2) <u>Extrinsic motivation</u> can also be really effective.
   Rewards or praise about your performance can make you feel <u>good</u> about yourself — so you're more likely to <u>want</u> to perform well again.

3) Most people are motivated by a <u>combination of both</u> types of motivation.

Official CGP tug o' war champion

Motivation Benefits Sports Performers in Different Ways

Increased Participation

1) To increase many areas of your fitness, you need to commit a large amount of <u>time</u> and <u>energy</u> to exercise.

2) People who are motivated are more likely to <u>participate</u> in exercise <u>regularly</u>, despite how much time and hard work it takes.

Maintained Training and Intensity

1) Motivation helps you to exercise at a <u>high intensity</u>, despite feeling <u>tired</u>.

2) You're more likely to work at <u>maximum capacity</u> and <u>complete</u> a training programme.

Improved Performance

1) People who are motivated are more likely to <u>train regularly</u>, which will help them to improve their <u>skills</u> at a particular sport.

2) This will improve their <u>performance</u> in <u>competitions</u> and <u>matches</u>.

Increased Fitness

1) Motivated sports performers are more likely to stick to a <u>training programme</u> and exercise multiple times a week.

2) This increases their <u>fitness</u>.

Motivation and Goal Setting

Goal Setting Can Help You Train

1) Goal setting means setting targets that you want to reach so you can improve your performance.

2) Goals can be short-term or long-term. Short-term goals are set over a period of 1 day to 1 month and are usually steps on the way to long-term goals, which can take months or years to complete.

3) Sports performers set goals to increase and direct their motivation.

4) Goal setting can influence motivation by:

- Giving you something to work towards — you are motivated to work hard to achieve your goal.

- Helping you to maintain focus on your task and monitor your progress. If you can see that the training is working, you are more likely to carry on.

- Boosting your confidence — reaching a goal can give you a sense of achievement.

Goal Setting Should be SMARTER

Personal goals need to be SMARTER:

S	**Specific**	➡ Say exactly what you want to achieve, e.g. 'My goal is to swim 1000 m continuously'.
M	**Measurable**	➡ Goals need to be measurable so that you can see how much you've progressed, e.g. 'My goal is to run 100 m in under 12 seconds'.
A	**Achievable**	➡ You need to make sure your goal is set at the right level of difficulty. If a target's too easy, it won't motivate you. If it's too difficult, you might start to feel negative about your performance, and give up.
R	**Realistic**	➡ It's important to make sure you have everything you need to reach your goal. This could mean having the right level of fitness and skill, or having enough resources (time, money, facilities...).
T	**Time-related**	➡ Set a deadline for reaching your goal. This makes your target measurable and keeps you motivated.
E	**Exciting**	➡ You need to enjoy working towards your goal and should want to achieve it.
R	**Recorded**	➡ Your achievements should be written down so that you can see how you are progressing towards your goal.

Chocolate biscuits — an effective form of extrinsic motivation...

There's a really handy way to remember what 'intrinsic' and 'extrinsic' motivation mean. 'Intrinsic' starts with 'in', so it comes from inside you. 'Extrinsic' starts with 'ex', just like 'exit', so it comes from outside.

About the Exam

Great job — you've made it to the end of the book. Here is what is in store for the <u>exam</u>...

You'll Sit One Exam

1) The exam will be based on what you've learnt about in <u>Component 3</u> of the course.
2) It'll be worth <u>60 marks</u> and will last <u>1.5 hours</u>.
3) It also makes up <u>40%</u> of your total grade.

Component 3 builds on what you've learnt in Components 1 and 2, so you'll need to use what you've learnt in these components in the exam too.

There Are Multiple-Choice Questions...

If you don't know the answer to a question, guess. You don't lose marks for putting a wrong answer.

You're given a choice of <u>possible answers</u> to the question.

The question tells you <u>how many answers</u> you need to give.

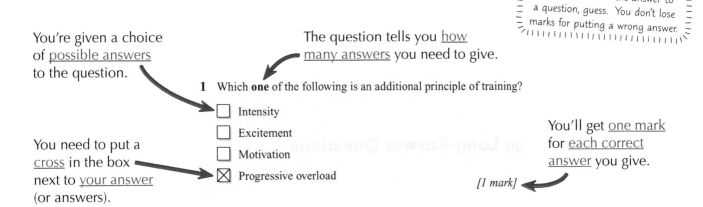

1 Which **one** of the following is an additional principle of training?

☐ Intensity

☐ Excitement

☐ Motivation

☒ Progressive overload

[1 mark]

You need to put a <u>cross</u> in the box next to <u>your answer</u> (or answers).

You'll get <u>one mark</u> for <u>each correct answer</u> you give.

...and Short-Answer Questions

In some short-answer questions, you may need to <u>apply</u> your knowledge to a <u>scenario</u>.

This question is asking you to '<u>explain</u>', so you need to give a reason then write about <u>how</u> or <u>why</u> it applies.

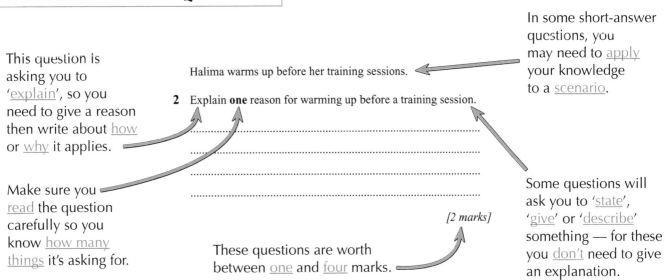

Halima warms up before her training sessions.

2 Explain **one** reason for warming up before a training session.

....

....

....

....

[2 marks]

Make sure you <u>read</u> the question carefully so you know <u>how many things</u> it's asking for.

These questions are worth between <u>one</u> and <u>four</u> marks.

Some questions will ask you to '<u>state</u>', '<u>give</u>' or '<u>describe</u>' something — for these you <u>don't</u> need to give an explanation.

About the Exam

Some Questions Involve Matching

You need to match each picture to the correct fitness training method by drawing a line.

Toby is a basketball player. He trains to improve his performance.

The scenario might help you — think about the components of fitness that a basketball player would want to improve.

3 Draw a line between each image and the fitness training method it shows.

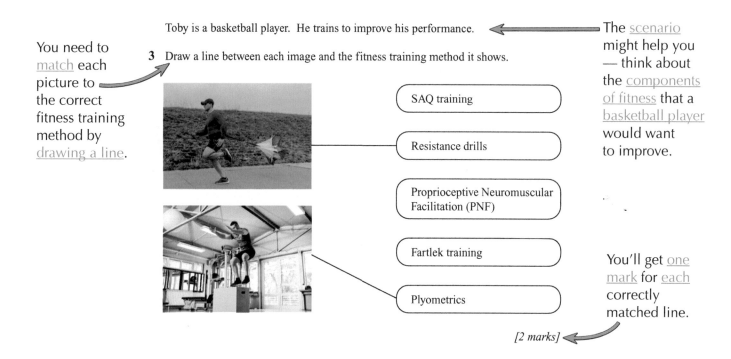

- SAQ training
- Resistance drills
- Proprioceptive Neuromuscular Facilitation (PNF)
- Fartlek training
- Plyometrics

You'll get one mark for each correctly matched line.

[2 marks]

There Will Also be Long-Answer Questions

'Evaluate' means you'll need to write about something from different points of view — e.g. the advantages and disadvantages of each type of provision.

4 Evaluate the effectiveness of public and private provision fitness clubs for sports performers.

....
....
....
....
....
....
....
....
....
....
....

Some questions might say 'assess', which is similar to 'evaluate'. You'll need to identify relevant factors and come to a conclusion.

[6 marks]

They're worth a whopping six marks.

You've put in the training — now for the main event...

Now you've read through the whole book, draw a mind map of all the information you can remember. Then flick back through each section, adding more detail to areas you missed or found particularly tricky.

Index

Index

J2RB1